It has been frequently, and truly, remarked by historians of her literature that Spain's most outstanding writers and thinkers have been, at the same time, men of action. In Spain the creative artist has usually forsworn temptation to immure himself in a "tower of ivory," therefrom to gaze in aloof contempt at the "profane multitude" below. Cervantes is, in this respect, perhaps the most typical of Spanish writers. "The courtier's, scholar's, soldier's eye, tongue, sword," all these were his, yet he knew poverty, disgrace, neglect, injustice, and shook them by the hand. Prosperity he never knew, and when fame, at long last, came knocking at his door, he was too old and weary to care much about the long awaited call.

There is, nevertheless, scarcely a trace of resentment or bitterness in his work. He never believed that "fine feathers make fine birds," and would, if alive to-day, surely be the first to endorse the sentiment that "there's nothing worth the wear of winning but laughter and the love of friends."

Among the great creative geniuses of the world Miguel de Cervantes is the most human, the most "clubbable," and the most lovable.—*L. B. Walton*

THE LIVING THOUGHTS LIBRARY
Edited by Alfred O. Mendel

CERVANTES

THE LIVING THOUGHTS LIBRARY

MIGUEL DE CERVANTES : A SELF-PORTRAIT. 1613

" He whom you here behold with aquiline visage, chestnut hair,
smooth and unruffled brow, merry eyes, and a nose arched, but well-
proportioned, a beard, silver, although golden not twenty years ago,
a large moustache, small mouth, teeth of no importance, for he has
but six of them and those in poor condition and worse placed because
they do not correspond with one another, the body between two
extremes, neither large nor small, complexion high, rather fair than
dark ; somewhat heavy in the shoulders, and not very nimble on his
feet ; this, I say, is the portrait of the author of the *Galatea* and *Don
Quixote of la Mancha.* . . ."

(From the Prologue to the *Exemplary Novel*)

CERVANTES

THE LIVING THOUGHTS OF

CERVANTES

Miguel de *(handwritten)*   Saavedra *(handwritten)*

PRESENTED BY

L. B. WALTON

Leslie Bannister *(handwritten)*

CASSELL

AND COMPANY, LIMITED

LONDON, TORONTO, MELBOURNE
AND SYDNEY

MOTTEUX's celebrated English rendering of *Don Quijote de la Mancha* is available in Messrs. J. M. Dent's Double Volume Series (London, 1933).

While his translation leaves much to be desired in the matter of exactitude, it is of considerable literary merit and has the advantage of being easily accessible to the general reader. The extracts presented have, therefore, been taken from this edition of Motteux. Some slight modifications in favour of greater accuracy have occasionally been introduced.

The excerpts from the *Novelas Ejemplares* are taken, by kind permission of Messrs. Gowans & Gray Ltd., from the English rendering by Norman Maccoll (*Complete Works of Miguel de Cervantes Saavedra*, ed. J. Fitzmaurice-Kelly, Vols. VII and VIII, Glasgow, 1902), again with certain modifications. The passages from the *Galatea* are from the English translation by Oelsner and Welford (Vol II in above series).

The extracts from the other works represented in this anthology appear in an English rendering of my own.

The *Don Quixote* references are to Dent's Motteux, Part, Book, and Chapter, thus : D.Q. 1. 4, xxv.

Readers should note that the division of Part I into Books is not observed in all editions of *Don Quixote*.

In the case of *Persiles and Sigismunda*, references are to Book and Chapter of the Spanish edition by Schevill and Bonilla (2 vols., Madrid, 1914). The title of the story is given in the case of the *Exemplary Novels*, and the name of the play in that of *Eight Comedies and Eight Interludes* (Spanish ed., Schevill and Bonilla, Madrid, 1918).

The following abbreviations have been used : D.Q. = *Don Quixote* ; P.S. = *Persiles and Sigismunda* ; E.N. = *Exemplary Novels* ; C.I. = *Eight Comedies and Eight Interludes* ; G. = *Galatea*.

The portrait of Cervantes which is reproduced as a frontispiece to this volume is only " traditional." A discussion of its claims to authenticity is to be found in James Fitzmaurice-Kelly's *Life of Cervantes* (Spanish translation, Oxford, 1917) and in various monographs by Spanish authorities.

L. B. WALTON

FIRST PUBLISHED IN GREAT BRITAIN 1948

PRINTED IN GREAT BRITAIN BY
MORRISON AND GIBB LTD., LONDON AND EDINBURGH
F. 1246

MIGUEL DE CERVANTES SAAVEDRA

BY

L. B. WALTON

I

THE MAN

1. The Eaglet is born

It has been frequently, and truly, remarked by historians of her literature that Spain's most outstanding writers and thinkers have been, at the same time, men of action. In Spain the creative artist has usually forsworn the temptation to immure himself in a " tower of ivory," therefrom to gaze in aloof contempt at the " profane multitude " below. Cervantes is, in this respect, perhaps the most typical of Spanish writers. "The courtier's, scholar's, soldier's eye, tongue, sword," all these were his, yet he knew poverty, disgrace, neglect, injustice, and shook them by the hand. Prosperity he never knew, and when fame, at long last, came knocking at his door he was too old and weary to care much about the long-awaited call.

There is, nevertheless, scarcely a trace of resentment or bitterness in his work. He never believed that " fine feathers make fine birds," and would, if alive to-day, surely be the first to endorse the sentiment that " there's nothing worth the wear of winning but laughter and the love of friends." Among the great creative geniuses of the world, Miguel de Cervantes is the most human, the most " clubbable," and the most lovable.

Although some of his admirers have invented impressive genealogies for him, his earliest traceable forbear is his great-grandfather, Rodrigo de Cervantes. We know that Rodrigo lived for a time at Cordova, and that he married Catalina de la Vera, or Cabrera. Their son Juan, who became a country lawyer, had three children, and one of these, Rodrigo, became the father of Miguel. Rodrigo de Cervantes was a doctor-surgeon of the type then common in Europe, a man of little education and narrow outlook who practised the primitive techniques of bleeding and purging so well thought of in those days. He married Leonor de Cortinas, and Miguel, number four in their family of seven, was baptized at Alcalá de Henares, in the Church of Santa María la Mayor, on the ninth of October 1547.

2. The Eaglet spreads his wings

While we have fairly ample information about his early manhood and middle age, not much is known concerning the youth of Cervantes. It is practically certain that he had little schooling of a conventional kind. On his own later showing, however, he was a fanatical lover of books. He tells us that, if better material were lacking, he would even pick up pieces of paper in the street on the chance of finding something to read. It is obvious from his writings that Cervantes had devoured a great many novels of chivalry. He was also well acquainted with the works of a number of Italian poets and with those of his Spanish contemporaries. The Spanish ballads were well known to him and, as lovers of Don Quixote will remember, he delights in quoting, paraphrasing, and " guying " them.

The young Miguel may have occasionally accompanied his father on the latter's rounds. We know that he used to watch performances by bands of strolling players, and it is to him that we owe an early description of the primitive equipment of theatrical touring companies at this period. Like so many other men of genius, Cervantes never understood where his true bent lay. It may be that his unfulfilled ambition to become a great dramatist took root at this early stage in his career.

His first known literary effort is a sonnet dedicated to Philip II's third wife, Isabel de Valois, and other poems by him appear in a collection published on the occasion of her death in 1568. This collection was edited by a Madrid schoolmaster, Juan López de Hoyos by name, who twice refers to Cervantes as his " beloved pupil." This fact has given rise to a widespread belief that Cervantes may have acted for a time as assistant in the school of which López de Hoyos was principal.

3. THE EAGLE SOARS AND IS MAIMED

In December 1569 Cervantes was in Rome, where he eventually became chamberlain to Cardinal Giulio Acquaviva. Speculation as to his reasons for leaving Spain has been, and is still, rife. It has been suggested that he was sentenced to exile and mutilation (in this case the loss of his right hand) on account of injuries received by an opponent in an affray.

The affair is, however, still obscure. This period of residence in Italy is of the utmost significance in the life of Cervantes. He then acquired sufficient knowledge of Italian to read the major Italian authors in the original, and Italian culture was a perpetual delight and inspiration to him. He writes in glowing terms of the surpassing beauty of Rome and Florence. This, indeed, was for him a period of intellectual and spiritual re-birth. Italy set an indelible mark upon him and the influence of the Greek and Latin classics worked upon him mainly through Italian poets and critics. Although, as we shall see later, he was by no means the " lay genius " (*ingenio lego*) portrayed by some of his admirers, he probably knew very little, if any, Greek, and had only a superficial knowledge of Latin. His main cultural inspiration was Italian, Spanish, and classical through Italian and Spanish media.

In 1570 he enlisted in the army, serving in the company commanded by Diego de Urbina. On 7th October 1571 he took part in the famous battle of Lepanto and was wounded in his left hand, sustaining a permanent injury. This wound won for him the honourable nick-name of " the cripple of Lepanto " (*El manco de Lepanto*).

He writes proudly of this episode in his Prologue to the *Exemplary Novels* (*Novelas Ejemplares*). Cervantes also took part in the operations before Navarino (1572), and Tunis (1573). He was later garrisoned at Palermo. Promotion being still a long way ahead, he decided to try his fortunes in his native country, armed with letters of introduction from Don John of Austria and the Duke of Sessa, the Viceroy of Naples. In

September 1573 he and his brother, Rodrigo, set out for Spain
on board the galley *El Sol*.

4. THE EAGLE IS CAGED

The ship was attacked by Moorish pirates and many of the
travellers, including Cervantes, were taken into captivity. The
letters from Don John of Austria and the Viceroy of Naples
which were in the possession of Cervantes naturally led his
captors to assume that he was a " very important person."
They therefore made up their minds to demand a heavy ransom
in his case. His imprisonment lasted five years, and during this
time he made no fewer than five attempts to escape, two of which
would have succeeded had it not been for the treachery of a
companion. His family eventually contrived to get together
a sum of money and entrusted it to two monks who were in
the habit of negotiating the ransom of Christian slaves. The
monks were much more interested in the fate of a certain
Jerónimo Palafox, but the absurdly large ransom demanded for
the latter led to the money being used for the release of
Cervantes.

His experiences as a captive undoubtedly made a profound
impression upon him, and provided material for various works,
including a play dealing with the life of a Christian slave in
Algiers.

5. THE EAGLE RETURNS

In December 1580 Cervantes was back in Spain and found
himself confronted with the problem which has faced the
returned warrior throughout the ages. How was he to provide
himself with a " home fit for a hero " ? What was he to do
for a living ? A grateful country made no answer. Those
years which, through no fault of his own, the locusts had eaten
could not be restored to him. It was not easy to begin life
over again at the age of thirty-three, however honourable the
scars one bore.

After his return from Algiers it is probable that Cervantes
was in Portugal for a time on some short-lived mission. He
failed, however, to obtain anything like a permanent job. In

those days it was even more difficult to make ends meet by writing than it is in our own times, especially if one had no influential patron to launch one upon what, in any event, was a precarious career. Cervantes had amused himself during his captivity by writing plays for the entertainment of his fellow prisoners. He tried his hand at poetry and wrote a pastoral romance, *Galatea*, the first part of which was probably concluded by 1585. The second part never materialized. He managed, however, to raise a small sum by selling the first part outright.

In December 1584 he married Catalina de Palacios Salazar y Vozmediano, his junior by eighteen years. The couple do not seem to have been much together during the early years of the marriage. The occupations of Cervantes encouraged a roving mode of life and it may be that his natural daughter by Ana Franca de Rojas was born at about this time.

He was now making a name for himself as a writer of "occasional" verse, and composed a number of dedicatory poems. To this period we may, perhaps, ascribe the "twenty or thirty" plays which he tells us he wrote "within about five years." Only two of these plays survive, *The Dealings at Algiers* (*El Trato de Argel*) and *Numantia* (*La Numancia*). In the former play one of the characters is called Saavedra and is, apparently, intended to be a self-portrait of the author.

6. THE EAGLE DROOPS AND DIES

After his father's death in 1585 Cervantes found himself with a mother and sister as well as a wife to support. For him patriotism had proved most decidedly "not enough." He was obliged to look out for a more settled source of income than that which the writing of "occasional" verse, plays, and romances could provide. He eventually managed to obtain employment as a Commissar in connection with the equipment of the "Invincible" Armada. His job was to requisition wheat and oil, and he did not distinguish himself in what was, to him, thoroughly uncongenial work. After the defeat of the Armada in 1588 he went to Seville as Commissar to the galleys, a job which he loathed even more than the previous one. After an unsuccessful attempt to obtain a post in America, he went back to the dreary routine of requisitioning, combined with the collection of taxes. Cervantes was a born financial muddler and found himself continually at loggerheads with his superiors. On one occasion he was imprisoned for carelessness in keeping his accounts and was eventually dismissed for incompetence. One can well believe that the dismissal was justified. Creative artists, and even mere scholars, are seldom good business men.

Between 1595 and 1603 Cervantes led a life of wretched poverty in Seville, turning out occasional verse from time to time.

+He was at Valladolid from 1603 to 1604 in response to a summons arising out of financial difficulties. In the latter year he obtained a licence for the publication of the First Part of *Don Quixote*, and the book appeared at Madrid in January 1605. We do not know, however, exactly when and where it was written. It has sometimes been hailed as one of the world's great " prison books," composed while its author was in gaol. This claim is doubtful. Nevertheless, part of the work may have been written while Cervantes was incarcerated at Seville or Argamasilla de Alba. The book seems to have been known prior to its publication, for the great playwright Lope de Vega, a rival and enemy of Cervantes, makes a contemptuous reference to it in a letter dated August 1604.

Lope de Vega could, however, do nothing to prevent it from enjoying an instantaneous success. Four editions were published in Spain during the year 1605.

In the same year, against a background of sordid poverty, general wretchedness, and what the Scots call " stair-head gossip," there occurred a mysterious episode in the life of Cervantes. He was charged with complicity in the murder of one Gaspar de Ezpeleta, who had been wounded outside the house in which Cervantes was lodging at Valladolid. Certain statements prejudicial to his daughter, Isabel de Saavedra, were made by a witness of the affair. This aspect of the matter was suppressed by biographers and their policy of " hush-hush " has led people unjustly to suspect that Cervantes may have connived at his daughter's illicit relations with a Portuguese, Simón Méndez.

In 1609 Cervantes joined a religious confraternity called "The Slaves of the Most Holy Sacrament," and made the acquaintance of the Count of Lemos, a personal contact which was to prove of considerable value to him. It was, however, also a source of disappointment. When Lemos was appointed Viceroy of Naples in 1610 a number of Spanish writers were invited to accompany him to that city. Cervantes was not among them, and he appears to have regarded the omission as a slight.

Twelve short stories, the *Exemplary Novels* (*Las Novelas Ejemplares*), were published in 1613, and in the following year the *Journey to Parnassus* (*El Viaje del Parnaso*) appeared. *Eight comedies and eight interludes* (*Ocho comedias y ocho entremeses*) saw the light in 1615. In 1614 a sequel to *Don Quixote*, attributed on the title page to one Alonso Fernández de Avellaneda, appeared at Tarragona. The name of the author was thought to be a pseudonym and the authorship of the book has been attributed to, among others, Lope de Vega, Tirso de Molina, and Ruiz de Alarcón, all celebrated playwrights of that age.

Goaded by the sneers and insults in the Preface to this spurious sequel, Cervantes finished the authentic Second Part, which appeared in 1615. Of all his further literary projects, and there were many, only *The Trials and Peregrinations of Persiles and Sigismunda* (*Los Trabajos de Persiles y Segismunda*), published posthumously in 1617, ever saw the light.

Cervantes now enjoyed a considerable reputation in Spain and his works were also fairly well known abroad. We know that the officials of the French Embassy in Madrid made enquiries about him. The only information they could obtain was that he was "old, a soldier, a gentleman, and poor." [1] His health failed in his declining years and the dedication of *Persiles and Sigismunda* to the absent Duke of Lemos reveals a tired and rapidly ageing man who, nevertheless, is still full of hope and courage.

He died on 23rd April 1616. His remains were interred in the Trinitarian Convent at Madrid. No monument or plaque marks the place of his burial.

---

[1] *Vide* Jas. Fitzmaurice-Kelly, *A New History of Spanish Literature.* (Oxford Univ. Press, 1926), to which I am indebted throughout this section.

II

THE AGE

1. The Moral "Atomic Bomb"

As is our own, the age of Cervantes was a period of change and unrest in almost every department of human activity. Standards and beliefs hitherto accepted as incontrovertible because they were regarded as finally established by an inspired and inerrant authority were then being blown as chaff before the wind of Renaissance humanism on the one hand, and the Protestant Reformation on the other. The latter, it is true, merely substituted an inerrant Book for an inerrant Church ; yet in its emphasis upon the significance of the individual and his direct personal relationship with the Deity ; in the stress which it laid upon the importance of the individual conscience as a valid guide upon the road to spiritual fulfilment, it worked, although unwittingly, in the same direction as the rationalistic and pagan humanism which was exhorting mankind to accept life rather than deny it, to live fully and freely, uninhibited by the Christian sense of sin.

If it had been pushed, as it was not, to its logical conclusion, the Protestant challenge might well have attained the same goal as that of rationalistic humanism. Even apparently devout Catholics did not remain wholly unaffected by the new spirit or, perhaps one should rather say, the ancient but revitalised Hellenic spirit of free enquiry and full living which was at that time enjoying a second manifestation in Italy.

Many passages in the works of Cervantes and other Spanish writers of his age suggest the Renaissance humanist rather than the devout and orthodox son of the Church. It would, however, in the writer's view, be quite unwarrantable to regard the author of *Don Quixote* as a kind of crypto-pagan or crypto-rationalist. He emerges, rather, as a believer who prefers not to scrutinize

8

too closely, and who is willing to leave theology to the theologians.

As we shall see later, it was rash, indeed, at that time for a Spaniard to risk collision with the most efficient " Gestapo " the world has ever known, the secret service of the Holy Inquisition. Spaniards who found the intellectual field unbearably restricted frequently sought refuge abroad, especially in Italy, where the climate of opinion was not quite so sultry. The more accommodating among them remained at home, making the best terms they could with the Church and with their consciences.

It must be borne in mind that the action of the " moral bomb " was a delayed one. All the implications of the great intellectual and spiritual unheaval of that age were not realized by those who witnessed its beginnings. It is we, to-day, who are receiving the full impact.

2. The Will of God. The Church and the Inquisition

(a) The Church, " Holy, Roman, Catholic, and Apostolic "

In an age like our own, critical, sceptical, scientific, and, at present, highly suspicious of all authoritarian claims, religious or political, an age which is rapidly throwing overboard the final remnants of orthodox Christian dogma, it is necessary to remind ourselves that the Churchmen of the time of Cervantes had, not only clear beliefs, but also clear consciences with regard to their intolerance of any beliefs other than their own.

It has been observed that there is, for Catholics, no such thing as a " fundamental " problem of life. The object of man's existence is, for them, clearly defined. The same was true, to a large extent, of orthodox Protestants in the age of Luther and Calvin. Like the Church for the Catholics, the Bible for the Protestants " knew all the answers." Protestantism, however, with its emphasis upon liberty of conscience, eventually gave rise to a bewildering variety of beliefs, none of which, until fairly recently, was especially remarkable for its tolerance.

The end and purpose of man, here and hereafter, have, for the Catholic, been revealed by God Almighty in Holy Writ

and, directly, by Jesus Christ, the Incarnate Son of God, who
founded his Church upon the apostle Peter. The Pope, in
direct line of succession to St. Peter, is believed to be the
" Vicar of Christ " on earth, and was declared, in 1870, to be
" infallible " when speaking *ex cathedra* for the purpose of
defining doctrine concerning faith or morals.[1] In this secular
age it is, one feels, necessary to outline very briefly the main
doctrines of the Roman Catholic Church and to emphasize the
fact that they were accepted as literally true by a large proportion
of civilized mankind during the period under discussion. It is,
indeed, impossible to understand the age of Cervantes without
some knowledge, however superficial, of this doctrine. The
Church, then, teaches : that God created the Universe out
of nothing ; that the first man and woman, Adam and
Eve, were created in order that they might enjoy a state of
eternal bliss, but that they disobeyed the command of God not
to eat of the fruit of a certain tree in their earthly Paradise, the
Garden of Eden. The precise nature of the act of disobedience
as described, or symbolized, in this Biblical story is not clearly
defined. Many theologians have, however, agreed that it had
something to do with the misuse of the sexual instinct, or the
arousing of that instinct. Eve tempted Adam, and he " fell."
In that Fall the whole of the human race is involved and because
of it merits eternal punishment. Human beings would, indeed,
all be damned eternally were it not for the grace of God and
the freely co-operating will of man.

Before co-operation with the grace of God could take place,
infinite goodness and infinite justice alike demanded an infinite
retribution for man's offence. Such a retribution finite man
could not supply, so God sent into the world his Only-Begotten
Son, Jesus Christ, the Second Person of the Holy Trinity, to
offer himself as a bloody sacrifice, a " ransom for many," by
submitting to an agonizing death on the Cross.

Prior to his death, and after his miraculous resurrection from
the dead, Jesus Christ taught the truth to his apostles.

Outside the Church founded upon St. Peter there is no
salvation (*Extra ecclesiam nulla salus*). The normal road to

[1] An excellent brief survey of this topic is to be found in George Bernard Shaw's
Preface to *St. Joan*.

membership of the Church is through the sacrament of Holy
Baptism administered by an ordained priest. In certain circumstances, however, it may be administered by a person in
minor orders, or even a layman, and those who, through no
fault of their own, have not been baptized, and who have
attained the age of reason, may, it is taught, possibly be saved by
what is known as the "Baptism of Desire." Unbaptized infants
cannot possibly enter Heaven. At one time it was generally
believed that such infants went to Hell, but they are now
presumed to go to the "Limbo of the Unbaptized." Virtuous
pagans who lived before the time of Christ go, it is generally
believed, to a special Limbo.

The other sacraments of the Church are Confirmation, Holy
Communion, Holy Matrimony, Holy Order, Penance, and
Extreme Unction (*i.e.* anointing of the sick, or dying, with
holy oils).

The activities of the Church on earth are not confined to
preaching the truth. Her priests, in direct succession to the
apostles, are believed to perpetuate in time the sacrifice of Christ
on the Cross. This they are alleged to do by means of the
Mass, the central act of worship of the Catholic Church. In
the Mass the bread and wine, symbolizing the bread and wine
of which Christ and his disciples partook at the Last Supper,
are believed to become, after consecration by the priest in due
form, the actual Body and Blood of the Redeemer. These,
it is held, are "really, truly, and substantially" received by
the faithful in Holy Communion. Controversy was rife for
centuries, and is still rife among theologians, as to the precise
nature of this miraculous change in the "Elements," as the
Sacred Host (unleavened bread in the form of a wafer, after
it has been consecrated by the priest) and the consecrated
wine are called. It was for long taught that the "accidents,"
i.e. the outward appearances or "sense data," remained unchanged and that only the "substance," that which underlay
the "accidents," was transformed. This doctrine, although still
favoured in some quarters, is bound up with a conception of
the nature of matter which is now outmoded. It was developed,
especially, by St. Thomas Aquinas from the teaching of the
Greek philosopher Aristotle, and has been dramatized with

magnificent lyrical symbolism in many religious plays by Calderón de la Barca and other Spanish playwrights.

The allegorical religious drama survived in Spain, as a living *genre*, well on into the eighteenth century, whereas in most other European countries it ceased to be a vital force after the close of the Middle Ages.

Perhaps the most important Catholic doctrine from our point of view is the much misunderstood teaching with regard to the "Power of the Keys." This particular doctrine was the immediate cause of the disruption which led to the Reformation. The Church teaches that there are three possible *post-mortem* destinations for human beings : Heaven, Purgatory, and Hell.

At one time the latter was regarded as the almost inevitable fate of the greater part of mankind, including, even, the majority of the clergy ! The teaching of the Church in this respect has, however, tended to become less stern. Many Catholic theologians to-day hold that few people, if any, will be condemned to eternal torment. We must, however, bear in mind, if we are to understand the moral climate of the age of Cervantes, that Hell was then regarded as a terrible reality. The Church still teaches that a person who dies unrepentant in a state of "mortal sin " will go to Hell, however virtuous he, or she, may have been in life. He, for example, who, having led an irreproachable life, chooses to play golf one Sunday morning rather than attend his obligatory Sunday Mass, and who has the misfortune to be run over and killed instantaneously before he has time to repent, cannot, in theory, escape Hell.[1] Catholic doctrine divides sin into two main classes, " mortal " and " venial." It would be out of place here, and beyond the writer's capacity, to discuss problems of moral theology. In order, however, to understand the doctrine of the " Power of the Keys," which so greatly influenced the thoughts and actions of men in the age of Cervantes, we must make it clear that, according to Catholic belief, a certain amount of " temporal " punishment is due for sin even after God has forgiven it and remitted its strictly just punishment of eternal damnation.

God, through his instruments, the priests of the Church, forgives sins, and the Church has inherited from the apostles

[1] But the Church teaches that there are " uncovenanted mercies."

this power to "bind and loose," in the Sacrament of Penance. In the early Church severe penances, such as pilgrimages, scourging, and the repetition of prayers throughout long periods, were imposed for the remission of the balance of " temporal " punishment still due for the sin, but the Church could, by granting an " Indulgence," remit all, or part, of the amount of such punishment due. Later, when severe penances were no longer customary, the extent of an " Indulgence " or pardon was often assessed with reference to the number of days of canonical penance which would formerly have been exacted in order to obtain remission of a part of the " temporal " punishment due for the sin. Hence the term *e.g.* " A 100 days Indulgence." A " Plenary " Indulgence remits *all* the temporal punishment due. There can be little doubt that many laymen of the age of Cervantes interpreted these Indulgences as meaning " 100 days (*etc.*) less in Purgatory " or, in the case of a " Plenary " Indulgence, " no Purgatory at all." A thriving trade was done in pardons by both genuine and alleged emissaries of the Pope, and St. Peter's, Rome, was erected, at any rate in part, upon the proceeds of such pardons. Catholicism tends to emphasize the importance of faith and contrition rather than " good works." Even though he may have been a rascal all his life, a man who dies " in a state of grace," armed with a valid Plenary Indulgence, is believed to go straight to Heaven.

As Baptism is believed to wipe out all stain of sin, people were wont at one period in the history of the Church to defer their baptism until they were gravely ill, or dying. Such a practice has been for long obsolete and its efficaciousness was always open to grave objections on the ground of *mala fides*.

Nevertheless, we must always bear in mind that Catholicism lays greater stress upon faith, repentance, and the efficacy of the sacraments than upon philanthropy and humanitarianism. It has been well said that there is no man more abhorrent to the good Catholic than the " lay saint," the virtuous agnostic or atheist. To the Church, the worst Catholic sinner who repents and dies " in a state of grace " is preferable in the eyes of God to the agnostic, however virtuous the latter may have been. This important aspect of Catholic teaching is well brought out in many Spanish religious plays, especially in Calderón's

Devotion to the Cross (La Devoción de la Cruz). The hero of this work, an abandoned criminal, is, nevertheless, saved in the end because of his lifelong devotion to the symbol of the Christian faith, and, of course, his ultimate contrition.

(b) The Inquisition

It will be readily understood from the foregoing that in the age of Cervantes life on earth was regarded by the faithful as of comparatively small significance. It was, indeed, merely an " antechamber to eternity." The Inquisition is, surely, the most outstanding example in human history of the evil which may sometimes be wrought by pure and disinterested motives. Holding the view of life which they did, there can be little doubt that the majority of the Inquisitors were sincere and honest men, with what they conceived to be the welfare of humanity at heart.

Those who may be inclined to doubt this statement should read, or re-read, the Preface to Mr. Bernard Shaw's *St. Joan,* where they will find a fair and objective account of the Inquisition and its methods. Every human institution has its blackguards and there were, no doubt, a number of sadists among the Inquisitors. Nevertheless, pity for the unrepentant heretic was almost certainly their predominant emotion. It must be borne in mind that the State regarded heresy, with its disintegrating effect upon national unity, as a criminal offence and, upon conviction by the inquisitorial tribunal, heretics were handed over to the State for punishment, with a formal recommendation to mercy. The usual penalty was death by burning. The latter was, however, frequently preceded by strangulation. Those who have the stomach for horrors, and who, in our times, have not, will find a moving account of an *auto da fe* in Enrique Larreta's famous historical novel *La Gloria de Don Ramiro.*[1]

Just as those who live under totalitarian régimes in our own day are subjected to tests of political orthodoxy and constant espionage by the secret service of the State, so, in the age of

[1] English translation, *The Glory of Don Ramiro,* by L. B. Walton. Dent, London, 1924.

Cervantes, Spaniards lived in a continual state of apprehension. Wives were set to spy on husbands, husbands upon wives, children upon parents. The accused was never confronted with his, or her, accuser. The whole procedure in the case of trials for heresy suggests, indeed, the now familiar techniques of totalitarian "justice." All authoritarian systems must, of necessity, provide an ideology and, if totalitarian, they seek to enforce this ideology upon the entire population. The main difference between the State-approved Inquisition and the tribunals of modern totalitarian régimes, appears to be that the upholders of the Inquisition sincerely believed that they were the instruments of the Divine Will. The element of cynical opportunism which characterizes the machinations of modern dictators was, in most cases, absent, nor was there any principle at work comparable with that which is embodied in the slogan "my country, right or wrong." The ethics of the Inquisition were consistent and, if one accepts the premises with regard to the nature and mission of the Catholic Church, entirely logical. Few to-day, even among Catholics themselves, seem to appreciate the inexorable and terrible logic of the Inquisition. The late Monsignor Hugh Benson, in his once widely read novels *The Lord of the World* and *The Dawn of All*, endeavoured to show that the Catholic Church, if it ever again won power, would be logically bound to re-introduce the Inquisition and permit the State, on occasions, to impose even the death penalty for heresy. It seems, however, most unlikely that Europe will ever be Catholic again in the sense that Spain was Catholic in the age of Cervantes. The possibility of another kind of dictatorship, intellectual and political rather than religious, must, however, be taken into consideration. A scientific, political, and financial oligarchy, armed with the atomic bomb, might well come to hold the world in thrall.

The issue is, indeed, portentous, as a study of the Inquisition in the age of Cervantes will show.

3. The Mind of Man. The World, the Flesh, and the Devil

(a) The World

Historical legends take an "unconscionable time a-dying" and none has enjoyed greater longevity than that which is known in Spain as "the Black Legend" (*La Leyenda Negra*). During the nineteenth century it was propagated in English-speaking countries by Prescott, Lea, Froude, and Buckle. Spain, we were assured, was "shut out from the light" while the rest of Europe basked in the vivifying beams of the rising sun of the Renaissance. Spain was presented as the most bigoted, priest-ridden and generally backward country in Europe. The outstanding achievements of Spaniards in the drama and the novel, the unsurpassed magnificence of Spain's pictorial art, were almost entirely ignored. Already, in the eighteenth century, the French essayist Montesquieu was saying that the only good book written by a Spaniard had merely served to show how ridiculous all the others were. A veritable hag's chorus of vilification chanted throughout Europe the same monotonous refrain. Spain was the pariah of Western culture. Nothing good had ever come, and nothing good could ever come, out of her. *Don Quixote* was a brilliant accident, its author an inspired idiot. And so on, and so forth.

Those old enough to remember the last two world wars were brought up in this tradition and it is not yet entirely dead. Its falsity is, however, being recognized more and more widely as the study of the Spanish language and Spanish literature develops in schools and universities outside the bounds of Spain. We most of us realize now that Spanish literature and thought were profoundly influenced, not merely by the revival of learning but also by the Reformation in general, and the works of Erasmus in particular.

We must never forget that the Spanish Moslems, whose civilization during the Middle Ages can compare favourably with that of any other European nation at the same period, kept the light of ancient culture alive and transmitted Arabic renderings of Aristotle to Renaissance Europe.

As early as the fifteenth century, Spanish poets and men of letters had made contact with the cultures of Italy and Provence. There was, indeed, a classical tradition in Spain before the coming of the Renaissance proper. Relations with Italy were especially close. Part of that country eventually came under Spanish rule, and many Spanish writers, including, as we have seen, Cervantes himself, visited it and were profoundly influenced by its culture. Twenty universities were established in Spain during the sixteenth century, including the famous University of Salamanca, which became a centre of the new learning and, together with Alcalá de Henares, the birthplace of Cervantes, could boast about ten thousand students.

A famous Spanish scholar and humanist, Juan Luis Vives (1492–1540), was for a time a Professor at Oxford. Miguel Servet, a Catalan, was a pioneer in research which eventually led to the discovery of the circulation of the blood. His condemnation as a heretic was due not, be it remarked, to the Inquisition, from which he sought refuge in Geneva, but to John Calvin. Many Spanish "intellectuals" sought, as we have seen, a freer mental climate in Italy and elsewhere. Others, however, possibly with certain "mental reservations," continued to live and work in Spain.

During the seventeenth century, the brilliant and subtle intellect of Schopenhauer's favourite Spanish author, Baltasar Gracián (1601–1658), found its expression in works of a decidedly secular and courtly stamp. Comparisons have frequently been made between certain works of Gracián and the *Maxims* of La Rochefoucauld. The latter may, indeed, owe something to the Spanish writer. The similarity of tone is startling, and those who are inclined to think of the genius of Spain as being essentially spontaneous, naïve, and untutored will certainly revise their opinion after reading such writers as Gracián, Quevedo, and Huarte de San Juan. The work of these authors is far too inadequately known outside the borders of their native land.

So far as scientific research is concerned, the view that the Church ever objected to it *as such* is erroneous. Many men of science, indeed some of the most eminent, have been Catholics. The Church joins issue with science only when the latter

challenges, openly or by implication, the authorized view of
man and the universe. The term "authorized view" demands
some explanation. For example, the main objection once
raised by the Church to the heliocentric view of the cosmos,
as opposed to the geocentric, was that the "heliocentricians"
cast doubt upon the picture of the universe revealed by God in
Holy Writ and the tradition of the Church. It was thought
by theologians in the age of Cervantes that revealed truth was
bound up with a world-picture in which the earth figured
as the most important of the heavenly bodies. It seemed,
therefore, only logical that it should occupy in the cosmos the
central position which had been allotted to it by pre-Copernican
"science." The Church has, of course, long ago abandoned
this position. It was, however, unfortunate for people like
Giordano Bruno and Galileo that she did not depart from it
earlier ! Her claim that her doctrine has remained unchanged
since the days of the apostles is not now held to extend to
scientific world-pictures, and it is admitted that the Pope himself
is just as likely to hold erroneous views in respect of such
pictures as you or I. The Pope is, indeed, as we have seen, held
to be "infallible" only when he defines, *ex cathedra*, doctrine
concerning faith or morals.

That the Church herself was influenced to no small extent
by the Reformation, and by Renaissance humanism, is hardly
open to doubt. The action, however, of these influences was
delayed. Our own "climate of opinion" is very different from
that of the Renaissance, so much so that we now tend to employ
the same terms in an entirely different sense. Theologians and
philosophers of those days wanted to make the universe con-
form to a system, to render it clear and intelligible to man, to
explain it. To-day, however, we realise that an explanation is
always in terms of some special mode of activity and that an
object may very well be one thing to, say, a painter, and quite
another to a mathematical physicist. We shall see later that
Cervantes had more than an inkling of what was then a new
or, rather, a renewed conception (for we find it among the
Greeks) of reality.

The modern mind has almost ceased to ask questions beginning
with "why" and confines itself almost exclusively to those

beginning with "how." For the rest, we are content to subscribe to the old slogan of the medieval schoolmen : *Omnia abeunt in mysterium.*

The researches of Copernicus had introduced man to an odd kind of world in which he felt bewildered and insignificant. He wanted to contact some rational element behind phenomena and his anthropomorphizing tendencies led him eventually to look for a " law " in nature, just as the theologians had sought for the human qualities of "justice," " mercy," and " benevolence " in God. For a time scientists and philosophers contrived to reach a none too comfortable accommodation with theology by admitting the existence of two kinds of " law " and two kinds of " truth," the natural and the supernatural. This distinction, be it noted, is one of the fundamental conceptions of Catholicism. The latter extends it even to such qualities as " goodness " and "justice." There is, so Catholics maintain, a " natural " goodness which may be the attribute of a pagan or an agnostic. Man is not, according to this view, *wholly* bad (as the Calvinists and the Scottish Church [1] conceive him to be) in spite of the " Fall." " Natural " goodness is, however, as nothing when compared with " supernatural " virtue as manifested, although unequally, in the persons of Jesus Christ, the Blessed Virgin Mary, and the Saints. For the men of those days there were, indeed, two distinct " worlds," two distinct " orders " of being, the natural and the supernatural. If we grasp this notion firmly and succeed in absorbing it (a difficult task in our day) we shall have gone far to understand the mentality of this age, so remote, intellectually and spiritually, from our own but which has, nevertheless, so many points of contact with it. Although, as we have seen, Spain did not escape the all-pervading influence of Renaissance humanism and the Protestant Reformation, she may rightly be regarded as the European representative *par excellence* of Catholic culture. This aspect of her national genius appears at its best in the work of her religious poets and in the theatre of Calderón de la Barca. In his *autos sacramentales,* religious plays of superb lyrical beauty, Calderón has dramatized in symbolic form the outstanding doctrines of the Catholic religion. His *Great*

Vide : The Westminster Confession of Faith.

Theatre of the World (*El Gran Teatro del Mundo*) shows us how life appears to a devout son of the Church, and handles, from an orthodox Catholic point of view, the then popular conception of the world as a vast stage upon which all human beings are " merely players." Other religious plays by Calderón deal with the mystery of transubstantiation and other dogmas of the Church. His most famous secular play, *Life's a Dream* (*La Vida es Sueño*), of which there is an English translation by Edward Fitzgerald,[1] is entirely Catholic in its atmosphere and teaching. In the past, religious prejudice has probably accounted for the comparative neglect of Calderón in English-speaking countries.

Nowadays, however, only a bigot would deny that European civilization owes much to Catholic thinkers, writers, scholars, and scientists. The work of Calderón is, in consequence, becoming better known, and the danger to-day lies rather in the direction of over-esteem than the reverse. It would surely be a mistake to return to the uncritical eulogies of the brothers Schlegel, who, during the romantic revival in Germany, hailed Calderón as " greater than Shakespeare " ! He remains, after all has been said in his favour, a local rather than a universal genius, exception being made of one or two plays such as the aforementioned *Life's a Dream*, *The Wonder-Working Magician* (*El Mágico Prodigioso*), and *The Mayor of Zalamea* (*El Alcalde de Zalamea*).

In order to be comfortable in the age of Cervantes it was, for a Spaniard, " above all things necessary to hold the Catholic faith." If one did not, and was vocal about one's unbelief, the eternal torment in Hell which the Church promised the unbeliever was likely to be preceded by an agonizing death on earth, just as in our own times political unorthodoxy in totalitarian states may involve torture and death in a concentration camp.

Between the age of Cervantes and our own, many striking comparisons can, indeed, be drawn. For religious bigotry read political intolerance ; for the secret service of the Inquisition read Gestapo, Ovra, or Ogpu ; for Jews and Moors read

[1] *Vide : Six Dramas of Calderón*, freely translated by Edward Fitzgerald. London, 1903.

" non-Aryans," and the parallel becomes clear. The Jews had, of course, been unpopular for a variety of reasons long before the sixteenth century. As the persecutors and murderers of Christ, the Middle Ages had dubbed them a " people of perdition," and to make matters worse they were racially akin to the Moslem invaders who had ruled over the major part of the Iberian peninsula for close upon seven centuries.

Forbidden to engage in " honourable " pursuits, such as a career in the army or at Court, and disliking manual labour, they resorted, especially, to usury as a means of livelihood. The lot of Moors and Jews in the age of Cervantes was by no means a happy one. The possession of Jewish or Moorish blood was regarded as a social disgrace and people were greatly concerned to obtain certificates of " purity of blood " (*limpieza de sangre*) in order to establish the absence of any such taint in their genealogy. There were various large-scale expulsions of Jews and Moors from Spain during the period under discussion. It has, however, been left to our own age to provide the most savage example of racial persecution in the history of mankind. That all the fault has invariably been on the side of the persecutors few would be prepared to maintain. Persecution on racial grounds alone is, however, clearly anti-Christian in principle, and it is, to say the least, odd that the Church not merely countenanced, but promoted and encouraged, the most ferocious pogroms and expulsions. In this matter the ethical teaching and policy of the Catholic Church has obviously changed, as the humanist would say, for the better. But the terrible fact remains that, given the validity of certain premises, persecution is logical and justifiable. " I beseech ye by the bowels of Christ," said Cromwell to the Levellers, " to reflect that perchance ye may be mistaken." Although Cromwell did not himself act up to his own maxim, it would have been well for the age of Cervantes if it had at that time been known and followed.

The resemblances between that age and our own are, however, not all on the debit side. The discovery and development of the New World, with its tremendous significance for the future of mankind, and the new scientific theories of Copernicus, may be compared with the scientific and technological developments of our own times. Aviation, the "wireless," and the new world-picture provided by the mathematical physicists have opened up vistas as pregnant as any of those revealed by Copernicus, Galileo, and the explorers of the new continent.

In the hierarchy of virtues in the age of Cervantes, loyalty to the King came immediately after obedience to the Church. As in the Middle Ages, temporal rulers were regarded as holding their possessions in a kind of divinely ordained trust. In spiritual matters, the Pope was, of course, supreme, and he also claimed, as the "patrimony of Peter," sovereign temporal rights over certain territory. Loyalty to the person of the monarch came to be a fetish, especially among the Spanish nobility of the so-called "Golden Centuries." It is the central theme of many Spanish plays and is one of the keynotes of Spain's great age of cultural achievement. Criticism of the existing social order was, however, by no means absent, and even the Church itself was not altogether immune from it.

The fact that *Lazarillo of Tormes* (*El Lazarillo de Tormes*, 1554), a little masterpiece of satirical portraiture which was, on several occasions, banned by the Inquisition, could, nevertheless, enjoy a fairly wide circulation, is evidence as to the strength of this dissentient element.

(b) The Flesh

An age which regarded the most heinous sins as being of the mind and spirit rather than of the body did not, as might be expected, take a very serious view of "straight fornication." Even homosexuality, although it is described by the Church as a "sin crying to Heaven for vengeance," seems to have been fairly common. Cervantes, Lope de Vega, and many other famous writers of the day, not to mention nobles and eminent ecclesiastics, had illegitimate offspring. Nobody appears to have thought much the worse of them for that. Spain, indeed, formed no exception to the general European rule. In England, no less a person than Cardinal Wolsey had openly kept mistresses, while the Popes were at one time notorious for the sexual irregularity of their lives. The records indicate that brothels did a flourishing business in Spain, as elsewhere. Behind a façade of rigid morality so far as marriage was concerned, the

Church seems, on the whole, to have been merciful to the sins of the flesh. In this it could, of course, point to the example of its Founder, whose teaching, as recorded in the New Testament, condemns pride and hypocrisy far more severely than concupiscence. Divorce was, and still is, anathema to Catholics. Nevertheless, the grounds upon which a Catholic marriage can be *annulled* are more numerous than those upon which a divorce can be obtained in the civil courts of England and Scotland.[1]

The position in the age of Cervantes seems to have been pretty much what it is now. Given the necessary money (the procedure was, normally, expensive) and, of course, a case which could be brought within the scope of the rules laid down by Canon Law, it seems to have been a fairly simple matter to get a marriage annulled. Separation *a mensa et thoro* (" from board and bed ") has always been permitted by the Church. As in the Middle Ages, concubinage, even where the clergy were concerned, seems to have been fairly common and rather a matter for jesting than for grave censure, at any rate on the part of the laity. The nobility, in Spain as elsewhere, frequently appear to have subscribed to the spirit of the doggerel slogan :

> " Honest toil and adulation
> Leave to them of low estate,
> Gambling, drink, and fornication
> Are the pastimes of the great,"

which, in one form or another, seems to have held good throughout the ages. As the brothers Quintero recently put it, through the mouth of a character in one of their most charming plays, *The Centenarian* (*El Centenario*) :

> "When the poor man gets drunk he's a drunken sot
> When the rich man gets drunk, what a humour the
> gentleman's got ! " [2]

Taboos have been relative not merely to time and place but also to social station.

Marriage, however, was hedged about with many restrictions,

[1] *Vide : Nullity of Marriage,* Mgr. P. E. Hallett (C.T.S., London, 1936).
[2] *Vide : A Hundred Years Old,* translated from the Spanish of Serafín and Joaquín Quintero by Helen and Harley Granville Barker, 1932.

at least so far as the wife was concerned. It has been said
that the " point of honour " (*el pundonor*) plays in the Spanish
theatre a part similar to that of Necessity in the drama of
ancient Greece. The idea of personal honour as conceived by
Spaniards of the " Golden Centuries " is far too complex a
subject with which to deal adequately here. Confining ourselves to matrimonial honour, we must bear in mind the fact
that marriage was regarded as a sacrament in which the
personalities of the husband and the wife were mystically and
indissolubly united. Thus a valid marriage, according to the
teaching of the Catholic Church, can never really be " dissolved,"
and a decree of nullity declares, in effect, that there has never
been a marriage at all. An offence to the wife was, therefore,
equally an offence to her husband. In degrading herself, she
degraded him. To debauch a man's wife was to offend his
honour in the gravest possible manner because, together with
this mystical notion concerning the union of personalities, there
was bound up the ancient Roman conception of the *paterfamilias*
and the *ius vitæ necisque* (power of life and death) which he at
one time had over the family. The wife was, from the purely
civil point of view, a kind of human chattel over which her
husband had definite rights.

In the age of Cervantes, a woman who tried to " live her
own life," and shirk her responsibilities to her husband and her
home, would have had an extremely uncomfortable time. In
those days a married woman had to exercise the utmost discretion if she wanted to " go off the rails." Much stress was
laid, then as now, upon the " eleventh commandment." An
injury to a man's honour as a husband could, in those days,
be wiped out only in blood, and frequently involved the death
of wife, lover, and (by suicide) the husband himself ! An injury
to the honour of a daughter or sister also demanded a bloody
vengeance on the part of father or brother. Such a situation is
admirably drawn for us by Calderón in one of his finest plays,
The Mayor of Zalamea (*El Alcalde de Zalamea*). It would be
unwise to lay too much stress upon a dramatic convention,
but there can be no doubt that the sexual " point of honour "
played a vital part in Spanish social life at that time.

(c) The Devil

Belief in God was by no means the only characteristic of the orthodox Catholic or Protestant in the age of Cervantes. As in the Middle Ages, the majority of Christians believed in the existence of a personal Devil. Luther, we are told, once threw an inkpot at him! One of Calderón's most famous plays, *The Wonder-Working Magician* (*El Mágico Prodigioso*), sometimes misleadingly called the "Spanish Faust," is mainly concerned with his activities. The Devil's trouble was pride, envy, and ambition. Once the highest of the angels, he had been passed over in favour of Man, for it was as a Man that God chose to incarnate his only Son. Resenting this choice, the Devil led a revolt against God and was eventually cast out of Heaven into the depths of Hell, where he reigns in sovereign wretchedness surrounded by evil spirits and damned souls. Great stress was laid in the age of Cervantes upon knowing one's place and keeping it. The fate of the Devil provided a salutary warning to the envious and ambitious. To obey, to submit, *perinde ac cadaver*, "after the fashion of a corpse," as St. Ignatius Loyola put it, was the supreme virtue; envy, the most ignoble vice. Whether the Devil really existed or not, he symbolized all that the authoritarian Church and State most feared and detested. He was a standing evil example to human beings, whom he delighted to tempt and lead astray.

Although now relegated to the background by most contemporary theologians, with the notable exception of the Anglican Mr. C. S. Lewis, he is still thought by many Catholics to be responsible for the phenomena of the séance room. In the age of Cervantes, belief in the Devil, familiar spirits, ghosts, witchcraft, and, especially, astrology, was practically universal, and such belief was by no means confined to Spain. Let us remember with shame and humility that the last "witch" was burned to death in Scotland as late as 1722! Belief in astrology is almost as common to-day as it was in the age of Cervantes and Shakespeare if, that is, we are to judge from the popular press.

4. The Mind of Cervantes

It must be made clear at the outset that Cervantes was no formal philosopher. For long, indeed, there flourished in Spain and elsewhere the notion that he was practically an ignoramus, a " lay genius " (*ingenio lego*), as some of his admirers have put it. In this connection it is interesting to observe that the same idea was for long current with regard to his great contemporary, Shakespeare. How such a notion could ever have gained general acceptance is one of the greatest enigmas in the history of literary criticism. One would imagine that the most cursory reading of Shakespeare and Cervantes must have clearly indicated that both these writers had, at least, a superficial knowledge of ancient history, literature, and thought, together with a smattering of Latin and, at least, one modern language other than their own.

Cervantes undoubtedly absorbed what was accessible to him in the contemporary climate of opinion, both in Italy and his native land. Although Calderón is of later date, to pass from him to Cervantes is to step intellectually from the Middle Ages to the threshold of the Renaissance. It is true that the " modernity " of Cervantes is frequently implicit rather than explicit. It is, nevertheless, a fact with which we have to reckon in any attempt adequately to assess his position in the hierarchy of Spanish letters.

His sympathy with what later came to be known as " biological determinism " is apparent in many passages of his works. Like Calderón, he is interested in the nature of reality and the tests by which the real can be distinguished from the illusory. Things, he asserts and implies repeatedly, are most certainly *not* what they seem.

Even Don Quixote himself, the great schizophrenic, in whom the world of fantasy and reality are so closely interwoven, eventually came to doubt whether his experiences in the magic cave of Montesinos were really authentic.

It is, indeed, possible to piece together, as Américo Castro has done in his masterly book on Cervantes,[1] a whole philosophy of life from this author's works. It is, however, in no sense a

[1] Américo Castro, *El Pensamiento de Cervantes*. Madrid, 1935.

formal or academic philosophy and, like most creative artists, Cervantes is, at times, inconsistent and even contradictory. Philosophically speaking, he is an amateur, the type of thinker beloved of the man-in-the-street, and, like the latter, much given to illogicalities. What especially endears him to the "common man" is his combination of rollicking, slapstick humour with subtle irony and wit; his detestation of prigs and humbugs; his hearty contempt for pedantry as distinct from genuine scholarship; his sympathy with the underdog; his love of animals; his fundamental democracy. Cervantes can laugh at, and see through, himself, a feat which comparatively few of his critics and expounders have, ostensibly, been able to perform. It is, indeed, probable that more solemn nonsense has been written about Cervantes than about any other great writer. Were he alive to-day, Cervantes would surely be the first to reject the extravagant claims made upon his behalf by some of his admirers.

Intellectually, he was a child of the Renaissance in Italy and Spain. Morally, he drew his ethical inspiration from neo-Stoicism rather than orthodox Christianity. In this, indeed, he is typically Spanish. Cervantes, if we except a few "common form" references to the doctrines of Holy Church, is, to judge by his works, a purely "human" moralist. It is not that he is actively hostile to religion or to the Church. Indeed, the contrary is the case. He prefers, however, to follow a different path from that indicated by Catholic orthodoxy, although this path may often appear to lead in the same direction. Attempts were made in Spain to reconcile Renaissance neo-Stoicism, which emphasized the self-rewarding character of virtue and put forward a fatalistic, pantheistic view of the universe, with orthodox Catholic doctrine. There is, however, little trace of this synthetizing tendency in Cervantes. He appears, if his works be reliable evidence, to accept the Stoic notion that man is the most important creature in the universe and that his reason is autonomous. For the Christian "obey the will of God" read "surrender yourself in obedience to your inevitable destiny"; for the Christian "bear patiently the ills which it is God's will that you should suffer" read "bear yourself in adversity like a man, and treat good and ill fortune alike," and

2

you have the central ethical teaching of the neo-Stoics. We are what we are because it is impossible that we should be otherwise. Let us, then, make the best of what may be an exceedingly bad job. Cervantes emphasizes again and again the immutability of individual character and temperament. " Sancho I was born, and Sancho I hope to die," remarks the squire in Part II, Chapter iv, of *Don Quixote*. It follows from this that both praise and blame are meaningless. You cannot expect an acorn to produce anything but an oak. This view of moral character as a biological product is in tune with certain modern conceptions.

The only genuine freedom, therefore, is the liberty which one has to follow the promptings of one's own personal dynamism. We are free, in effect, to do what we are bound to do. In situations of almost intolerable mental and physical agony man must accept his destiny, not merely with impassivity but *willingly*. The influence of orthodox Catholic teaching upon Cervantes is shown by the fact that he does not appear to accept suicide as a solution to intolerable ills. Release by death must remain in the hands of nature, conceived by Cervantes as the " majordomo " of God, a kind of demiurge. His attitude to warfare is especially interesting in view of recent improvements in the technique of slaughter. There can be no doubt whatever that he regarded the profession of soldiering as an honourable and worthy occupation to be ranked even higher than that of the scholar or the writer. He condemns, nevertheless, the use of artillery in warfare. Cannon are " devilish instruments whose inventor, I am satisfied, is now in Hell, receiving the reward of his cursed invention . . ." One wonders what Cervantes would have made of "Coventration," " saturation raiding " and the " atomic bomb " ! His views on the general perversity of human nature are well expressed in the fourth book of the *Galatea*, where he plaintively enquires : "What praiseworthy thing is there to-day in the world, however good it be, the use of which cannot be changed into evil ? "

It would, however, be misleading to stress the significance of Cervantes as a formal moralist. The wind of his genius blew where it listed, and he is " allergic " to docketing.

In the field of aesthetics we are on safer ground. So far as the theatre was concerned, Cervantes undoubtedly supported, at least in theory, the neo-classicists who aimed at developing a drama on the lines of that of Greece and Rome. It is true that he by no means always practised what he preached. Creative artists rarely do. It is obvious from his works that he was well acquainted with the " rules " of Aristotle's *Poetics* as interpreted, or distorted, by Renaissance commentators. He accepted the alleged distinction between " particular," *i.e.* historical, and " universal," *i.e.* poetic, truth, and stands firmly by the " law of the Unities." He approaches his great novel in the spirit of one who is about to write both history and poetry, and his continual references to *Don Quixote* as a " true history " (*verdadera historia*) are a tribute to his grasp of neo-classic principles. Nevertheless, that Sancho Panza is deliberately intended to symbolize " historical " or particular truth and his master " poetical " or universal truth, the writer must decline to believe.

When Cervantes has warmed to his work he forgets all about the theory of " verisimilitude " and the " imitation of nature." He becomes, indeed, a law unto himself and creates an entirely new *genre*, the modern novel.

III

THE WORKS

1. THE DRAMA

IN ORDER TO UNDERSTAND THE POSITION OF CERVANTES IN RE-
lation to the national theatre of Spain, we must bear in mind
that the latter owes little to the drama of Greece and Rome.
In this it resembles the English Elizabethan drama and differs
profoundly from the classical theatre of France. For a time,
however, the path which the Spanish theatre was to take
remained undecided. Some dramatists toyed with the pseudo-
Aristotelian " unities " of time, place, and action, so well
summed up by the French poet and critic Boileau in his
famous lines : " Qu'en un jour, en un lieu, un seul fait accompli
Tienne jusqu'à la fin le théâtre rempli." These playwrights, like
the neo-classical French dramatists, showed a preference for
themes taken from ancient history or mythology. Cervantes
associated himself at first with this school and, through the
mouth of the Canon in Don Quixote, adversely criticizes those
who ignore the dramatic unities of time, place, and action.
The theatre of Lope de Vega, his triumphant rival, is of an
entirely national character, Spanish through and through.
Lope cast all his weight on the side of the masses. The people,
he says, in effect, pay the piper, so they must be allowed to
call the tune. He tells us that he threw Plautus and Terence
aside before sitting down to write a play. Lope's almost
incredible fecundity, and the enormous popularity which his
plays enjoyed, gave the neo-classical theatre of Spain its coup de
grâce. Cervantes bowed to the inevitable. He seems, nevertheless, to have preserved a sneaking regard for the literary
technique of the ancients and the pseudo-Aristotelian rules.

Although he regarded the theatre as his most appropriate
métier, the plays of Cervantes are remembered because it

was he who wrote them rather than on account of their intrinsic merits. In his best, or perhaps one should rather say his least defective plays he can rise to heights of moving eloquence as, for example, in *Numantia* (*La Numancia*) which celebrates the defence of Numantia against the vast armies of the Roman general, Scipio Africanus. This play was much admired by the German romantics, and no less a person than the great Goethe himself praises it. During the recent Civil War in Spain it was revived, by both parties to the struggle, for purposes of propaganda and raising of morale.

2. THE EXEMPLARY NOVELS AND THE ROMANCES

(*a*) The *Exemplary Novels* (*Novelas Ejemplares*) appeared at Madrid in 1613. Cervantes here uses the term *novela* in the Italian sense of " short story " and claims, not without some justification, to have introduced this type of literature to his native country. It would, however, be out of place here to discuss the validity of a claim to originality which has been much disputed. It is now generally admitted that Cervantes owes a good deal to foreign sources.

His use of the adjective " exemplary " is interesting. This does not mean that he regarded the tales as of exemplary merit. He intends to convey that they were written with a moral end in view and is simply paying lip-service to the neo-classical idea that imaginative literature ought to have a serious purpose. The amoral nature of some of the tales has laid Cervantes open to accusations of hypocrisy. The lessons which they teach are, however, not in the nature of conventional platitudes. The stories everywhere reveal a profound understanding of human nature at both its highest and its lowest levels. The author brings to the brute facts of his own experience the sympathy, understanding, and urbanity of a thinker who is also a man of the world. In a story like *The Jealous Old Man* (*El Viejo Celoso*) he attempts, as we have seen, to vindicate the rights of nature and the normal sexual impulses as against the claims of a conventional and hypocritical moral code. We must, however, always bear in mind that his teaching is implicit rather than explicit. He is no tub-thumper, crank, or agitator. Nowhere does he openly attack or defy the doctrines of the Catholic Church. In his own words, his object was : " to set up in the market-place of our commonwealth a billiard table at which everyone can entertain himself without fear of injury, I mean without hurt to mind or body, because virtuous and agreeable exercises rather benefit than harm. It is so, for people are not always at Church, the oratories are not always occupied, men are not always taken up with affairs, however well qualified they may be for them. There are hours of recreation when the harassed spirit may rest." [1]

Of the twelve novels, *Rinconete and Cortadillo*, a dynamic picture of low life in Seville, *The Little Gypsy Girl* (*La Gitanilla*), and *The Dialogue of the Dogs* (*El Coloquio de los Perros*) are perhaps the most likely to please a modern reader.

The Exemplary Novels became well known outside Spain. Many of their themes were dramatized by non-Spanish playwrights, including Middleton and Rowley, Beaumont and Fletcher, Rotrou and Quinault. Fitzmaurice-Kelly thinks that the story of the little gypsy girl, Preciosa, may have influenced Victor Hugo's conception of Esmeralda. Sir Walter Scott admitted that he was first impelled to write fiction by reading the *Exemplary Novels*.

(*b*) The pastoral romance, *Galatea*, and the fantastic novel of adventure, *The Trials and Peregrinations of Persiles and Sigismunda, a Story of the North*, do not call for special mention. As a *genre*, the pastoral romance is even more tedious than the novel of chivalry and it cannot be said that the efforts of Cervantes in this field are very much better than those of other practitioners. *Galatea* is written in a pleasing, rhythmical, euphuistic prose, interspersed with eclogues. It is clear, however, from *Don Quixote* and, especially, the *Dialogue of the Dogs* that Cervantes was conscious of the basic absurdity of the *genre*. Sometimes he uses the conventional pastoral setting as a background for philosophical musings, as, for example, in the fourth book of *Galatea*, where he expounds the neo-platonic view of beauty as interpreted by the Spanish Jew, León Hebreo.

In the episode of Camacho's wedding (*Don Quixote*, Part II, Chapter xx) the idealistic pastoral trend is united with the

[1] *Vide* Preface to the *Exemplary Novels*.

realistic and the picaresque. That Cervantes lacked a serious interest in, and sympathy with, this type of literature is, however, indicated by the fact that he never troubled to write his promised second part of *Galatea*.

The Trials and Peregrinations of Persiles and Sigismunda, a Story of the North (*Los Trabajos de Persiles y Segismunda, historia septentrional*) appeared posthumously in 1617. "Trabajos," literally "works," is used here by Cervantes in a combination of two of its generally accepted senses at that time, to wit, "peregrinations," or "trials." The characters are as fantastic and unreal as the background of their activities. The latter rival the wildest exploits of the chivalric heroes. Fatal passions, enchantments, horoscopes, and so forth, play an important part in a work which would have been consigned to oblivion long ago had it not been written by the author of *Don Quixote*.

Unlike Lope de Vega, Cervantes pays little attention to the elaboration of dramatic intrigue. His theatre is one of character and passion rather than of plot. Influenced, possibly, by the allegorical religious drama which flourished in Spain right on into the eighteenth century, he was fond of introducing personified abstractions into his plays. The latter are, for the most part, ill-constructed and lack dramatic unity. Their interest is chiefly historical and, of course, personal. We do not willingly leave unread anything from the pen of the author of *Don Quixote*.

While he failed in the "full-dress" drama, Cervantes attained notable success as a writer of "interludes" (*entremeses*). These were short dramatic pieces designed to precede or follow the performance of a longer play, or to be performed during the interval between two acts of a play. Cervantes made use of a large variety of themes drawn from Spanish folklore and the works of Italian writers. These he elaborates with a subtle irony and wit not inferior to that which he exhibits in *Don Quixote*. He attacks, explicitly or implicitly, the foibles of various social classes and treats of matrimonial problems such as divorce, which, as we have seen, admitted of only one orthodox solution in those days. As a character in the *entremés* entitled *The Divorce Judge* (*El Juez de los Divorcios*) puts it, "better the worst reconciliation than the best divorce!"

In *The Jealous Old Man* (*El Viejo Celoso*) Cervantes makes us wonder whether incompatible marriages do not, in fact, constitute the worst kind of sexual immorality. In another piece, founded on an old folk tale, the author introduces us to a couple of rogues who are touring the country with a miraculous tableaux show. The characters in it are alleged to be invisible to converted Jews and bastards ! Many, in consequence, pretend to be vastly entertained by the non-existent figures !

The *entremeses* of Cervantes are well worth reading, and it is, indeed, surprising that they are so little known outside Spain.

3. THE ETERNAL QUIXOTE

What is there about this book that has so greatly endeared it to all ages and to all races, to young and old alike ? If the hallmark of a classic is universality of appeal in time and space, *Don Quixote* must surely be awarded a commanding place in the hierarchy of European letters. Voltaire, when asked his opinion of Dante's *Divine Comedy* is alleged to have replied, somewhat cynically : "*C'est un grand livre; personne ne le lit.*"

Of *Don Quixote* one might well say : " It is a great book ; everybody has read it." Children, and the simple-minded, love it for its rollicking, slapstick fun and as a great adventure story. It is, however, a book which grows on, and with, the reader. There is not only something in it for every age of the individual human being, but also for every age of history since the time of its composition. The eighteenth-century neo-classicists and the nineteenth-century romantics alike acclaimed it. It is always topical ; never more so than now when man is as puzzled and perplexed in the new universe to which he is being introduced by mathematicians and physicists, as was Don Quixote in his half-real, half-fantastic world. Modern man is, in effect, a worshipping animal who is in process of losing his faith. Like the Manchegan knight in his declining years, man is beginning to wonder whether he has not, after all, been deceived by fairy-tales. The fundamental schizophrenia of our times calls to that of the age of Don Quixote, and to that of Don Quixote himself.

The masterpiece of Cervantes has been enjoyed at one time
for its hearty fun and subtle irony ; at another as a burlesque
of the romances of chivalry ; at another for its skilful treatment
of the " master and man " theme. To-day, its chief appeal is,
I think, psychological. Sancho Panza's continual emphasis upon
the material and practical aspects of human existence has its
parallel in our contemporary utilitarianism. The first reaction
to any form of human activity to-day tends to take the shape
of the question : " But what is the *use* of it ? " Don Quixote
impresses the majority nowadays as being a tragic, foolish, and
pathetic figure. He is what *we* used to be when the fairy bells
still chimed for us and we lived with the hope of Heaven and
the fear of Hell. Don Quixote speculated upon the authenticity
of his experiences in the magic cave of Montesinos, and doubt
touched his heart with its gentle and chilly finger. Modern
man feels that *he* has emerged from *his* magic cave of Montesinos, the world of religious orthodoxy, into the light of science
and reason. He is almost convinced that he has been the victim
of a great illusion. Can he continue to live without another
such ? Or will the brutal materialism of our times, with its
enthronement of " go get " as the only rational aim in life,
lead him eventually to destroy himself with that crowning
glory of the scientific era, the atomic bomb ? When Don
Quixote recovered his sanity or, if one cares to put it in that
way, when his illusion died, he expired with it. Will the human
race follow his example ? A large-scale return to the old faith
and the old morality seems unlikely. Will man discover a new
faith, and a more rational moral code, or will he perish from
spiritual inanition ? The dilemma is an appalling one, and it is
interesting to note that one of the first European thinkers to
give clear expression to it was a countryman of Cervantes,
Miguel de Unamuno.[1]

While contemporaries of its author and, especially, eighteenth-
century readers, appear to have regarded the masterpiece of
Cervantes as, primarily, a comedy, it is rather as a tragedy that
it makes its appeal to our own generation. All great creative

---

[1] *Vide* Miguel de Unamuno, *El Sentimiento Trágico de la Vida en los Hombres y
en los Pueblos.* (English trans. by Crawford Flitch, *The Tragic Sense of Life in
Men and Peoples.* London, 1921) ; also *La Agonía del Cristianismo,* 1930.

writers appear to have sensed that the essence of tragedy is to be found at the point where the latter makes contact with the absurd.[1] During the past six years, both combatants and non-combatants in this second world war have been living at this junction. The continual proximity of the horrific and the ridiculous during agonizing "blitzes" has made civilians, as well as soldiers, conscious of the tragedy at the heart of comedy, and the comedy at the heart of tragedy. No creative writer has shown himself more acutely aware of this odd medley at the core of things than Miguel de Cervantes.

It is this sensitiveness to the tragi-comic element in life, this refusal either to take tragedy too seriously or comedy too lightly, which causes him to appear so surprisingly modern, if one may be pardoned for using an adjective so greatly abused in our times.

To take only one example, we might cite the episode of the unfortunate boy, Andrés, who is being flogged unmercifully by his master and whose temporary release Don Quixote secures only to bring more savage punishment upon the lad in the end. It is all very unfair and yet, somehow, extremely funny. And we can do nothing whatsoever about it. So, says Cervantes, better laugh than cry! "El mundo es así," thus wags the world. Whatever our destiny may be, it cannot be other than it actually is because we cannot be other than we actually are. Cold comfort, perhaps, but comfort nevertheless, as every true Stoic has found.

For those who find the conditions of human existence almost intolerable ; for those who have suffered, and are still suffering, hardship and injustice ; for those who abandon hope of discovering either a practical or a mystical solution to the eternal problems, Cervantes is, as the poet Rubén Darío puts it, "un buen amigo," a friend indeed, in times of disillusion and despair.

4. CONCLUSION

In conclusion, it is, perhaps, hardly necessary to point out that the compiler of an anthology such as this is bound to be influenced, to some extent, by his own personal conception of

[1] Cf. Américo Castro : op. cit.

the essential Cervantes. It was, for reasons of space, quite impossible to include every passage which appeared to throw light upon the Spanish writer's *Weltanschauung*. It must also be borne in mind that the views expressed in many of the extracts are placed by Cervantes in the mouths of his characters, and do not always necessarily represent his own settled opinion.

To the best of his knowledge and ability, and after more than thirty years devoted to the study of Spain and Spanish literature, the compiler has endeavoured to provide here a fair, all-round picture of a noble mind which, while it gave birth to no formal or highly original philosophy of life, penetrated to the depths, and scaled the heights, of our unhappy human nature.

L. B. Walton has selected the essence of the thought of
Cervantes from

DON QUIXOTE

THE EXEMPLARY NOVELS

EIGHT COMEDIES AND EIGHT INTERLUDES

THE TRIALS AND PEREGRINATIONS OF PERSILES AND SIGISMUNDA

GALATEA

KEY DATES IN THE LIFE OF MIGUEL DE CERVANTES SAAVEDRA

October 9, 1547	Baptized in the Church of Santa María la Mayor at Alcalá de Henares.
1569–70	In Italy. Chamberlain to Cardinal Giulio Acquaviva.
1570	Enlists in Spanish army.
1571	Wounded in the battle of Lepanto.
1573	Sets out for Spain in the galley *El Sol*.
	Captured by pirates.
1573–80	A prisoner in Algiers.
1580	Returns to Spain.
1584	Marries Catalina de Palacios Salazar y Vozmediano.
1585	Publication of *Galatea* (Part I).
1588	Officially appointed Commissar for equipment of Invincible Armada.
1593–1603	Life of extreme poverty in Seville.
1603–04	In Valladolid.
1605	The affair of Ezpeleta.
	Publication of *Don Quixote* (Part I).
1613	Publication of the *Exemplary Novels*.
1614	Publication of the *Journey to Parnassus*.
	Appearance of the spurious Second Part of *Don Quixote*.
1615	Publication of *Don Quixote* (Part II), and *Eight Comedies and Eight Interludes*.
April 23, 1616.	Death of Cervantes.
1617	Posthumous publication of the *Trials and Peregrinations of Persiles and Sigismunda*.

38

THE MAJOR SURVIVING WORKS
OF MIGUEL DE CERVANTES SAAVEDRA

(1547–1616)

(The titles in Spanish are given in brackets)

1585	First Part of *Galatea* (*La Galatea*).
1583–87 (?)	*Numantia* (*La Numancia*).
	The Dealings at Algiers (*El Trato de Argel*).
	Dates of these two plays unknown, but probably composed between 1583 and 1587, during which period Cervantes tells us that he wrote "twenty or thirty" plays.
1605	First Part of *Don Quixote* (*El Ingenioso Hidalgo Don Quijote de la Mancha*).
1613	The *Exemplary Novels* (*Las Novelas Ejemplares*).
1614	The *Journey to Parnassus* (*El Viaje del Parnaso*).
1615	Second Part of *Don Quixote*.
1615	*Eight Comedies and Eight Interludes* (*Ocho Comedias y Ocho Entremeses.*
1617	*The Trials and Peregrinations of Persiles and Sigismunda* (*Los Trabajos de Persiles y Segismunda*).

THIS SORRY SCHEME

Heaven can do whatever it likes without anybody being able to interfere with it, especially when it is raining.

C.I., *The Mayors of Dagaço.*

* * *

The losses and ills which are styled fruits of sin proceed from, and are caused by, ourselves.

E.N., *The Dialogue of the Dogs.*

* * *

We must leave the world in the state in which we find it.

C.I., *The Labyrinth of Love.*

* * *

Every man's nose will not make a shoehorn. Let us leave the world as it is.

D.Q., II, lix.

* * *

St. Peter is very well at Rome ; which is as much as to say, let every man stick to the calling he was born to.

D.Q., II, liii.

* * *

In this life desires are infinite in number and some are bound up with others and linked together so that they form a chain which may, perhaps, reach to Heaven or descend into Hell.

P.S., IV, x.

* * *

He that aims at things impossible ought justly to lose those advantages which are within the bounds of possibility.

D.Q., I, 4, vi.

* * *

There is no striving against the stream and the weakest still goes to the wall.

D.Q., I, 4, xx.

* * *

He that lives long suffers much.

D.Q., II, xxxii.

* * *

There is not a leaf on any tree that can be moved without the permission of Heaven.

D.Q., II, iii.

* * *

Let us leave all to Heaven, that knows all things that befall us in this vale of misery, this wicked, troublesome world, where we can be sure of nothing without some spice of knavery or imposture.

D.Q., II, ii.

* * *

The viper is not to be blamed for the poison with which she kills, seeing it was assigned her by nature.

D.Q., I, 2, v.

* * *

There is a remedy for all things but death.

D.Q., II, lxiv.

* * *

What praiseworthy thing is there to-day in the world, however good it be, the use of which cannot be changed into evil? Let philosophy be condemned, for often it discovers our faults, and many philosophers have been wicked; let the works of the heroic poets be burned, for with their satires and verses they reprehend vices; let medicine be blamed, for men discover poisons; let eloquence be called useless, for at times it has been so arrogant that it has placed in doubt the recognized truth; let not arms be forged, for robbers and murderers use them; let not houses be built, for they can fall upon the inhabitants; let variety of victuals be prohibited, for they are wont to be a cause of illness; let no one seek to have children, for Oedipus, driven by cruellest madness, slew his father, and Orestes smote the breast of his own mother; let fire be counted evil, for it is wont to burn houses and to consume cities; let water be despised, for with it all the earth was flooded; in a word, let all elements be condemned, for they can be perversely used by some perverse persons. And in this manner every good thing can be changed to evil, and from it can proceed evil effects, if placed in the hands of those who, like irrational beings, allow themselves to be governed by the appetite, without moderation.

G., Bk. IV.

* * *

Every beginning in anything is difficult.

G., Bk. III.

* * *

If lovers marked, as in the ancient custom, with white and black stones their sad or happy days, without any doubt the unhappy would be more.

G., Bk. IV.

* * *

Make yourself honey and the flies will eat you.

D.Q., II, xlix.

* * *

Every day produces some new wonder ; jests are turned into earnest and those who designed to laugh at others happen to be laughed at themselves.

D.Q., II, xlix.

. * * *

To think that the affairs of this life are always to remain in the same state is erroneous and a fallacy. The face of things rather seems continually to change and roll with circular motion ; summer succeeds the spring, autumn the summer, winter the autumn, and then spring again ; so time proceeds in this perpetual round ; only the life of man is ever hastening to its end, swifter than time itself, without hopes to be renewed, unless in the next, that is unlimited and infinite. . . . For even by the light of nature, and without that of faith, many have discovered the swiftness and instability of this present being, and the enduring quality of that eternal life which we await.

D.Q., II, liii.

* * *

It is the belly that makes the feet amble, and not the feet the belly.

D.Q., II, xxxiv.

* * *

What rare parts are lost to mankind for want of their being exerted and known !

D.Q., II, lxii.

* * *

Prudent men should judge of future events by what has taken place in the past, and what is taking place in the present.

P.S., II, vii.

* * *

If the astrologer is sometimes correct in his judgments it is because he relies upon what is most likely to occur, and upon what has happened on the majority of occasions.

P.S., I, xiii.

* * *

It is difficult to bear anguish of mind if the weakness of the body does not put forth all its strength.

P.S., I, i.

* * *

Tell me thy company and I will tell thee what thou art.

D.Q., II, xxiii.

* * *

When you see your friend, trust to yourself.

D.Q., II, xii.

* * *

Many important principles of prudence and morality have been learned from irrational creatures ; as the use of enemas from the stork, and the benefit of vomiting from the dog. The crane gave man an example of vigilance, the ant of providence, the elephant of honesty, and the horse of loyalty.

D.Q., II, xii.

* * *

Next to the elephant the dog holds the first place in the appearance of having understanding ; next the horse, and lastly the ape.

E.N., *The Dialogue of the Dogs.*

* * *

One way of defining man is to say that he is a laughing animal, because it is only man who laughs, and no other creature ; and I say that it can also be maintained that he is a weeping animal, an animal which cries ; and just as excessive laughter is the sign of a feeble intellect, so much weeping reveals a weakness in reasoning power. . . .

P.S., II, v.

* * *

Whether the pitcher hit the stone, or the stone the pitcher, it is bad for the pitcher.

D.Q., II, xliii.

* * *

The oak produces acorns ; the pear tree, pears ; the vine, grapes ; and the honourable man, honour, because none of them can do otherwise.

C.I., *The Miraculous Tableaux Show*.

* * *

Seasons and times are not always the same, but often take a different course ; and what the vulgar call forebodings and omens, for which there are no rational grounds in nature, ought only to be esteemed lucky hits, by the wise.

D.Q., II, lviii.

* * *

Eyes are deceived, for at first glance tinsel seems as good to them as gold ; but after a brief interval they well recognize the difference there is between the true and the false.

E.N., *The Little Gypsy Girl*.

* * *

Although hypocrisy is wont to walk very skilfully, the mask falls from it in the long run and it remains without the sought-for prize.

P.S., I, xxii.

* * *

O envy, envy ! thou gnawing worm of virtue, and spring of infinite mischiefs, there is no other vice but pleads some pleasure in its excuse ; but envy is always attended by disgust, rancour, and distracting rage.

D.Q., II, viii.

* * *

When a man is down, " down with him ! "

D.Q., II, lxviii.

* * *

Of all the sins that men commit, none is so great as ingratitude.

D.Q., II, lviii.

* * *

Hell is said to be full of the ungrateful.

D.Q., II, lviii.

* * *

Let him be a wretch who thinks himself one.

D.Q., I, 3, vii.

* * *

Fear is sharpsighted and can see things underground.

D.Q., I, 3, vi.

* * *

Too much of one thing clogs the appetite, but scarcity makes everything go down.

D.Q., II (Preface).

* * *

A fool knows more in his own house than a wise body in another man's.

D.Q., II, xliii.

* * *

He is a fool indeed, and a great fool, who, when imparting a secret to another, asks that other, with great earnestness, to keep silent about it because it is a matter of life and death to the teller that what he says should not be made known.

P.S., II, v.

* * *

The fool and the simpleton can neither gossip nor backbite : and although it is not good to speak evil well, the discreet backbiter meets with approval ; for no conversation fails to be rendered sharp and savoury by malicious wit, just as salt sharpens viands, and, if the witty backbiter is blamed and condemned as obnoxious, he is none the less absolved and praised as a clever fellow.

P.S., II, v.

* * *

The most difficult part in a play is the fool's, and therefore a fool must not attempt to write it.

D.Q., II, iii.

* * *

Even fools love authority.

D.Q., II, lxiii.

* * *

THE GOLDEN AGE

O happy age, which our first parents called the age of gold !
Not because gold, so much adored in this iron age, was then
easily purchased, but because those two fatal words *mine* and
thine were distinctions unknown to the people of those fortunate
times ; for all things were in common in that blessed age :
men, for their sustenance, needed only to lift their hands and
take it from the sturdy oak, whose spreading arms liberally
invited them to gather the wholesome savoury fruit ; while
the clear springs, and silver rivulets, with luxuriant plenty,
offered them their pure refreshing water. In hollow trees, and
in the clefts of rocks, the labouring and industrious bees erected
their little commonwealths, that men might reap with pleasure
and with ease the sweet and fertile harvest of their toils. The
tough and strenuous cork-trees did of themselves, and without
other art than their native liberality, dismiss and impart their
broad light bark, which served to cover these lowly huts,
propped up with rough-hewn stakes, that were first built as a
shelter against the inclemencies of the air. All then was union,
all peace, all love and friendship in the world ; as yet no rude
ploughshare presumed with violence to pry into the pious
bowels of our mother earth, for she, without compulsion,
kindly yielded from every part of her fruitful and spacious
bosom, whatever might at once satisfy, sustain, and indulge her
frugal children. Then was the time when innocent, beautiful
young shepherdesses went tripping over the hills and vales ;
their lovely hair sometimes plaited, sometimes loose and flowing,
clad in no other vestment but what was necessary to cover
decently what modesty would always have concealed. The
Tyrian dye and the rich glossy hue of silk, martyred and dis-
sembled into every colour, which are now esteemed so fine and
magnificent, were unknown to the innocent simplicity of that
age ; yet, bedecked with more becoming leaves and flowers,
they may be said to outshine the proudest of the vain-dressing

ladies of our age, arrayed in the most magnificent garbs, and all the most sumptuous adornings which idleness and luxury have taught succeeding pride ; lovers then expressed the passion of their souls in the unaffected language of the heart, with the native simplicity and sincerity in which they were conceived, and divested of all that artificial contexture, which enervates what it labours to enforce ; imposture, deceit, and malice had not yet crept in and imposed themselves unbribed upon mankind in the disguise of truth and simplicity : justice, unbiassed either by favour or interest, which now so fatally pervert it, was equally and impartially dispensed ; nor was the judge's whim law, for then there were neither judges nor causes to be judged ; the modest maid might walk wherever she pleased alone, free from the attacks of lewd, lascivious importuners. But in this degenerate age, fraud and a legion of ills infecting the world, no virtue can be safe, no honour be secure ; while wanton desires, diffused into the hearts of men, corrupt the strictest watches, and the closest retreats, which, though as intricate and unknown as the labyrinth of Crete, are no security for chastity.

D.Q., 1, 2, iii.

* * *

THE STATE, ITS RULERS, AND ITS CITIZENS

Slothful, lazy, lewd people in a commonwealth are like drones in a bee-hive, that waste and devour the honey which the labouring bees gather.

D.Q., II, xlix.

* * *

The ornament of a person that is advanced to an eminent post must be answerable to its greatness, and not debased to the inclination of his former meanness. Let thy apparel be neat and handsome : even a stick well dressed does not look like a stick . . . let thy dress be suitable to thy degree, and always clean and decent.

D.Q., II, li.

* * *

Laws not well obeyed are no better than if they were not made, and only show that the prince who had the wisdom and authority to make them had not the resolution to see them executed : and laws that only threaten, and are not kept, become like the log that was given to the frogs to be their king, which they feared at first, but soon scorned and trampled on.

D.Q., II, li.

* * *

New rulers, new laws.

D.Q., II, xlx.

* * *

Where the kings are, there are the laws.

D.Q., II, v.

* * *

There never lack those that will lend governors money when they have none.

D.Q., II, v.

* * *

Among the many other fatigues which royalty sustains, it is one of the greatest to be obliged to hear every one, and to give answer to all people.

D.Q., II, vi.

* * *

The laws of enforced obedience oblige us to do much : but those of our inclinations much more.

P.S., IV, i.

* * *

Truth to tell, I have it in mind to dissemble where rulers are concerned, for they have long arms and reach out wheresoever they wish, and to whomsoever they wish, and experience has already shown me that it is not well to offend the powerful, and Christian charity teaches that we must pray Heaven for the life and health of a virtuous ruler and, in the case of a bad ruler, that he may improve and amend his ways.

P.S., I, xiv.

* * *

The harsh and unconscionable actions of kings are baptized with the name of severity.

P.S., II, xiii.

* * *

Not all truths should appear in public, nor present themselves to the gaze of every eye.

P.S., I, xiv.

* * *

How many people in this world live without government yet do well enough, and are well looked upon ?

D.Q., II, v.

* * *

Neither learning nor any other abilities are very material to a ruler. Have we not a hundred of them that can scarce read a letter, and yet they govern as sharp as so many hawks.

D.Q., II, xxxii.

* * *

It is a dainty thing to command, though it were but a flock of sheep.

D.Q., II, xlii.

* * *

When the severity of the law is to be softened, let pity, not bribes, be the motive.

D.Q., II, xlii.

* * *

Every man ought to wear clothes suitable to his place and dignity ; for a lawyer should not go dressed like a soldier, nor a soldier like a priest.

D.Q., II, xlii.

* * *

It is easy to begin a business, but a hard matter to carry it through.

D.Q., II, xvi.

* * *

When the scale of justice is even, or a case is doubtful, we should prefer mercy before rigour.

D.Q., II, li.

* * *

Prudent judges punish, but do not exact vengeance for crimes ; discreet and pious judges mingle equity with justice, and give proof of their sound judgment by combining rigour with clemency.

P.S., III, x.

* * *

Merchants are greater in their shadows than in themselves, and as they only by a miracle attend to anything else than their traffics and contracts, they bear themselves modestly : and as ambition and wealth are eager to show themselves, they find an outlet for them in their sons, and so their fathers treat them and provide for them as if they were the children of a prince, and some there are who procure titles for them and contrive to place on their breasts the mark which distinguishes people of quality from the plebeians.

E.N., *The Dialogue of the Dogs*.

* * *

The inclination to steal and the act of stealing are, in thieves, inseparable concomitants that are never sundered except by death.

E.N., *The Little Gypsy Girl*.

* * *

No gipsy is ignorant, and no gipsy girl is dull ; for as they gain their livelihood by being acute, astute, and liars, they sharpen their wits at every step, and have no chance of becoming moss-grown. . . . there is not a child of twelve who does not know as much as if she were five-and-twenty, for their masters and preceptors are the devil and experience, which teach them as much in an hour as they would otherwise learn in a year.

E.N., *The Little Gypsy Girl*.

* * *

There are some men who busy their heads, and lose a world of time, in making discoveries, the knowledge of which is good for nothing on this earth, unless it be to make the discoverers ridiculous.

D.Q., II, xxi.

* * *

It lessens the value of praise to be the publisher of it oneself.

D.Q., II, xvi.

* * *

All the lineages and descents of mankind are reducible to . . . four heads : first, of those who, from a very small and obscure beginning, have raised themselves to a spreading and prodigious magnitude. Secondly, of those who, deriving their greatness from a noble spring, still preserve the dignity and character of their original splendour. A third are those who, though they had large foundations, have ended in a point like a pyramid, which by little dwindles as it were into nothing, or next to nothing, in comparison with its base. Others there are (and those are the bulk of mankind), who have neither had a good beginning nor a rational continuance, and whose ending shall be therefore obscure ; such are the common people, the plebeian race.

D.Q., II, vi.

* * *

Hunting wild beasts is the most proper exercise for knights and princes ; for in the chase of a stout, noble beast may be represented the whole art of war, stratagems, policy, and ambuscades, with all other devices usually practised to overcome an enemy with safety. Here we are exposed to the extremities of heat and cold ; ease and laziness can have no room in this diversion ; by this we are inured to toil and hardship, our limbs are strengthened, our joints made supple, and our whole body hale and active : in short it is an exercise that may be beneficial to many, and can be prejudicial to none . . .

D.Q., II, xxxiv.

* * *

DON QUIXOTE'S ADVICE TO SANCHO BEFORE THE LATTER TAKES UP HIS GOVERNORSHIP

Be well pleased with the meanness of thy family, nor think it a disgrace to own thyself derived from labouring men ; for, if thou art not ashamed of it thyself, nobody else will strive to make thee so. Endeavour, rather, to be esteemed humble and virtuous than proud and vicious. The number is almost infinite of those who, from low and vulgar births, have been raised to the highest dignities, to the papal chair, and the Imperial throne ; and this I could prove by examples enough to tire thy patience.

Make virtue the medium of all thy actions, and thou wilt have no cause to envy those whose birth gives them the titles of great men and princes ; for nobility is inherited, but virtue acquired : and virtue is worth more in itself than nobleness of birth.

If any of thy poor relations come to see thee, never reject or affront them ; but, on the contrary, receive and entertain them with marks of favour ; in this thou wilt display a generosity of nature, and please Heaven that would have nobody to despise what it has made.

If thou sendest for thy wife, as it is not fit a man in thy station should be long without his wife, and she ought to partake of her husband's good fortune, teach her, instruct her, polish her the best thou canst, till her native rusticity is refined to a handsome behaviour ; for often an ill-bred wife throws down all that a good and discreet husband can build up.

Shouldst thou come to be a widower (which is not impossible) and thy post recommend thee to a bride of higher degree, take not one that shall, like a fishing-rod, only serve to catch bribes. For, take it from me, the judge must, at the general and last court of judicature, give a strict account of the discharge of his duty, and must pay severely at his dying-day for what he has suffered his wife to take.

Let never obstinate self-conceit be thy guide ; it is the vice of the ignorant, who vainly presume on their understanding.

Let the tears of the poor find more compassion, though not more justice, than the informations of the rich.

Be equally solicitous to find out the truth where the offers and presents of the rich and the sobs and importunities of the poor are in the way. Wherever equity should, or may, take place, let not the extent or rigour of the law bear too much upon the delinquent ; for it is not a better quality in a judge to be rigorous than to be merciful.

When the severity of the law is to be softened, let pity, not bribes, be the motive.

If thy enemy has a cause before thee, turn away thine eyes from thy prejudice, and fix them upon the question of fact.

In another man's cause, be not blinded by thine own passions, for those errors are almost without remedy ; or their cure will prove expensive to thy wealth and reputation.

When a beautiful woman comes before thee, turn away thine eyes from her tears, and thine ears from her lamentations ; and take time to consider sedately her petition, if thou wouldst not have thy reason and honesty lost in her sighs and tears.

Revile not with words those whom their crimes oblige thee to punish in deed ; for the punishment is adequate for the wretches without the addition of ill language.

In the trial of criminals consider as much as thou canst, without prejudice to the plaintiff, how defenceless and open the miserable are to the temptations of our corrupt and depraved nature ; for though God's attributes are equal, yet His mercy is more attractive and pleasing than His justice.

.   .   .   .   .

As to the government of thy person and family, my first injunction is cleanliness. Cut thy nails, nor let them grow as some do, whose folly persuades them that long nails add to the beauty of the hand ; till they look more like beaver's claws than a man's nails. It is foul and unsightly. Keep thy clothes tight about thee ; for a slovenly looseness is a sign of a careless mind ; unless such a negligence, like that of Julius Caesar, be affected for some cunning design.

Prudently examine what thine income may amount to in a year ; and if sufficient to afford thy servants' liveries, let them be decent and lasting rather than gaudy and for show ; and for the surplus of thy good husbandry, bestow it on the poor. That is, if thou canst keep six footmen, have but three ; and let what would maintain three more be laid out in charitable uses. . . .

Lest thy breath betray thy peasant stock, defile it not with onions and garlic.

Walk with gravity, and speak with deliberation, and yet not as if thou didst hearken to thine own words ; for all affectation is a fault.

Eat little at dinner, and less at supper ; for the stomach is the storehouse whence health is to be imparted to the whole body.

Drink moderately ; for drunkenness neither keeps a secret nor observes a promise.

Be careful not to chew on both sides of thy mouth at once, that is, fill not thy mouth too full, and take heed not to belch before company.

When thou ridest, cast not thy body all on the crupper nor hold thy legs stiff down and straddling from the horse's belly ; nor yet so loose, as if thou wert still on thine ass ; for the air and gracefulness of sitting a horse distinguishes somewhat a gentleman from a groom.

Sleep in moderation ; for he that rises not with the sun loses so much day. And remember that diligence is the mother of good fortune ; sloth, on the contrary, never effected any thing that sprung from a good and reasonable desire. . . .

Never undertake to dispute or decide any controversies concerning the pre-eminence of families ; since, in the comparison, one must be better than the other ; for he that is lessened by thee will hate thee, and the other, whom thou preferest, will not think himself beholden to thee.

D.Q., ɪɪ, xlii and xliii.

* * *

Though sometimes those who govern are destitute of sense, yet it often pleases God to direct them in their judgment.

D.Q., ɪɪ, xlv.

* * *

THE PEN AND THE SWORD

There is no book so bad but something good may be found in it.

D.Q., II, iii.

* * *

He who publishes a book runs a very great hazard, since nothing can be more impossible than to compose one that may secure the approbation of every reader.

D.Q., II, iii.

* * *

To compile a history, or to write any book whatsoever, is a more difficult task than men imagine.

D.Q., II, iii.

* * *

A poet's pen is allowed to inveigh against envy and envious men ; and so against other vices, provided it aim not at particular persons.

D.Q., II, xvi.

* * *

There are poets so abandoned to the itch of scurrility that rather than lose a villainous jest they will venture being banished to the islands of Pontus.

D.Q., II, xvi.

* * *

The pen is the tongue of the mind ; the thoughts that are formed in the one, and those that are traced by the other, will bear a near resemblance.

D.Q., ii, xvi.

* * *

It is within the bounds of possibility that a workman should be a poet, for poetry does not reside in the hands, but rather in the understanding, and the soul of a tailor is just as capable of poetry as that of a Grand Master.

P.S., i, xviii.

* * *

One ought to treat poetry as a most precious jewel whose owner does not wear it every day, nor does he show it to all the world, nor at every step, only when the occasion is appropriate and there be reason for showing it. Poetry is a most lovely damsel, chaste, virtuous, lively, clear-sighted, retiring, and keeps herself within the limits of the most lofty discretion. She is a friend to solitude, fountains entertain her, meadows console her, trees free her from cares, flowers delight her ; finally, she charms and instructs all who have intercourse with her.

E.N., *The Little Gypsy Girl*.

* * *

There is not a poet who is not rich, since they all live content with their estate, a philosophy which few maintain.

E.N., *Ibid*.

* * *

Of a truth there are poets in the world who write stanzas that no devil can understand.

E.N., *The Illustrious Kitchen-Maid*.

* * *

History, poetry, and painting serve as symbols one of another, and are so alike that when you write history, you paint, and when you paint, you write history. History is not always of equal moment, nor does painting invariably depict great and portentous events, nor yet does poetry always speak in a celestial fashion. History admits lowly themes ; painting, weeds and broom, in its pictures ; and poetry, maybe, enhances its merits when it sings of humble matters.

P.S., III, xiv.

* * *

Do but take care to express yourself in a plain, easy manner, in well-chosen, significant, and decent terms, and to give an harmonious and pleasing turn to your periods : study to explain your thoughts, and set them in the truest light, labouring, as earnestly as possible, not to leave them dark nor intricate, but clear and intelligible : let your diverting stories be expressed in diverting terms, to kindle mirth in the melancholic, and heighten it in the gay : let mirth and humour be your superficial design, though laid on a solid foundation, to challenge attention from the ignorant and admiration from the judicious : to secure your works from the contempt of the graver sort and deserve the praises of men of sense.

D.Q., I (Preface).

* * *

Modesty is a virtue seldom found among poets, for almost every one of them thinks himself the greatest in the world.

D.Q., II, xviii.

* * *

Homer never wrote in Latin, because he was a Greek ; nor did Virgil write in Greek, for Latin was the language of his country. In short, all your ancient poets wrote in their mother-tongue, and did not look for other languages in which to express their lofty thoughts. And thus it would be well that this custom should extend to every nation, there being no reason that a German poet should be despised because he writes in his own tongue, or a Castilian or a Basque, because they write in theirs.

D.Q., ii, xvi.

* * *

Translation from one language to another, except it be from the noblest of tongues, the Greek and Latin, is like viewing a piece of Flemish tapestry on the wrong side, where though the figures are distinguishable yet there are so many ends and threads that the beauty and exactness of the work is obscured, and not so advantageously discerned as on the right side of the hangings. Neither can this barren employment of translating out of easy languages show either wit or mastery of style, no more than copying a piece of writing by a precedent : though still the business of translating wants not its commendations, since men very often may be worse employed.

D.Q., ii, lxii.

* * *

As in the time of the Romans all used to talk Latin as their mother tongue, there would be some foolish fellow among them whom his talking Latin would not prevent from being a fool.

E.N., *The Dialogue of the Dogs.*

* * *

There are some who suppose they know the Greek language without knowing it, as some pretend to Latin, though ignorant of it.

E.N., *Ibid.*

* * *

For knowing how to be silent in Spanish and how to talk in Latin there is need of judgment.

E.N., *Ibid.*

* * *

A silly remark can be made in Latin as well as in Spanish.

E.N., *Ibid.*

* * *

He who speaks Latin in the presence of him who is ignorant of it sins as much as he who employs Latin phrases although ignorant of them.

E.N., *Ibid.*

* * *

There are some whom their being Latinists does not save from being asses.

E.N., *Ibid.*

* * *

Certainly Aeneas was never so pious as Virgil represents him, nor Ulysses so prudent as he is depicted by Homer.

D.Q., ii, iii.

* * *

I do not much wonder at Orlando's being so very valiant, considering that he was enchanted in such a manner that he could not be slain but by the thrust of a long pin through the bottom of his foot, which he sufficiently secured, always wearing seven iron soles to his shoes.

D.Q., i, 3, xii.

* * *

Learning without virtue is like a pearl upon a dunghill.

D.Q., ii, xvi.

* * *

All affectation is a fault.

D.Q., ii, xliii.

* * *

Be brief, for no discourse can please when too long.

D.Q., 1, 3, vii.

* * *

Even the mountains breed scholars and men of sense.

D.Q., 1, 4, xxv.

* * *

I have known woods breed learned men, and simple sheep-cotes contain philosophers.

D.Q., 1, 4, xxiii.

* * *

The scribbling devil is (*of all imps*) the most irresistible. When that demon is got into a man's head he takes the possession for inspiration, and, full of his false ability, falls slapdash to writing and publishing, which gets him as much fame from the world as he has money from the booksellers, and as little money from the booksellers as he has fame from the world.

D.Q., ii (Preface).

* * *

Those glimmerings of genius that peep through the chinks of a narrow fortune have always gained the esteem of truly noble and generous spirits.

D.Q., ii (Preface).

* * *

TWO UNFORTUNATES : THE SCHOLAR AND THE SOLDIER

These, then, I say, are the sufferings and hardships a scholar endures : first, poverty (not that they are all poor, but to urge the worst that may be in this case), and having said he endures poverty, methinks nothing more need be urged to express his misery ; for he that is poor enjoys no happiness, but labours under this poverty in all its parts, at one time in hunger, at another in cold, another in nakedness, and sometimes in all of them together, yet his poverty is not so great, but still he eats, though it be later than the usual hour, and of the scraps of the rich, or, which is the greatest of the scholar's misfortunes, what is called among them " going a-sopping," neither can the scholar miss of somebody's stove or fireside to sit by, where, though he be not thoroughly heated, yet he may gather warmth, and at last sleep away the night under a roof. I will not touch upon other less material circumstances, as the want of linen, and scarcity of shoes, thinness and threadbareness of their clothes, and their surfeiting when good fortune throws a feast in their way. This is the difficult and uncouth path they tread, often stumbling and falling, yet rising again and pushing on, till they attain the preferment they aim at ; whither being arrived, we have seen many of them, who having been carried away by a fortunate gale through all these quicksands, from a Chair govern the world ; their hunger being changed into satiety, their cold into comfortable warmth, their nakedness into magnificence of apparel, and the mat they used to lie upon, into stately beds of costly silks and softest linen ; a reward due to their virtue. . . . But yet their sufferings, being compared with those the soldier endures, appear much inferior. . . . Let us now observe whether the soldier be anything richer than he ; and we shall find that poverty itself is not poorer ; for he depends upon his miserable pay, which he receives but seldom, or perhaps never ; or else in that he makes by marauding, with the hazard of his life, and the trouble of his conscience. Such is sometimes his want of apparel, that a slashed buff coat is all his holiday raiment and shirt ; and in the depth of winter being in the open field, he has nothing to cherish him against the sharpness of the season but the breath of his mouth, which, issuing from an empty place, I am persuaded is itself cold, though contrary to the rules of nature. But now see how he expects night to make amends for all these hardships in the bed prepared for him, which, unless it be his own fault, never proves too narrow ; for he may freely lay out as much of the ground as he pleases, and tumble to his content, without danger of losing the sheets. But, above all, when the day shall come, wherein he is to put in practice the exercise of his profession, and strive to gain some new degree ; when the day of battle shall come, then, as a mark of his honour, shall his head be dignified with a cap made of lint, to stop a hole made by a bullet, or be perhaps carried off maimed, at the expense of a leg or an arm. And if this do not happen, but that merciful Heaven preserve his life and limbs, it may fall out that he shall remain as poor as before, and must run through many encounters and battles, nay, always come off victorious, to obtain some little preferment ; and these miracles are too rare : but . . . how few are those who obtain due rewards in war in comparison with those numbers that perish ? . . . It is quite otherwise with scholars, not only those who follow the law, but others also, who all either by hook or by crook get a livelihood ; so that though the soldier's sufferings be much greater, yet his reward is much less.

D.Q., I, 4, x and xi.

* * *

Let none presume to tell me that the pen is preferable to the sword ; for be they who they will, I shall tell them they know not what they say ; for the reason they give, and on which chiefly they rely, is that the labour of the mind exceeds that of the body, and that the exercise of arms depends only on the body, as if the use of them were the business of porters, which requires nothing but much strength ; or, as if this, which we

who profess it call chivalry, did not include the acts of fortitude
which depend very much upon the understanding. Or else as
if that warrior, who commands an army or defends a city
besieged, did not labour as much with the mind as with the
body. If this be not so, let experience teach us whether it be
possible by any bodily strength to discover or guess the intentions
of an enemy. The forming designs, laying of stratagems,
overcoming of difficulties, and shunning of dangers, are all
works of the understanding, wherein the body has no share. It
being, therefore, evident that the exercise of arms requires the
help of the mind as well as learning, let us see in the next place
whether the scholar's or the soldier's mind undergoes the greatest
labour. Now this may be better known by regarding the end and
object each of them aims at ; for that intention is to be most valued
which makes the noblest end its object. The scope and end of
learning . . . is to give a perfection to distributive justice,
bestowing upon every one his due, and to procure and cause
good laws to be observed ; an end really generous, great, and
worthy of high commendation ; but yet not equal to that
which knight-errantry tends to, whose object and end is peace,
which is the greatest blessing a man can wish for in this life. . . .
This peace is the true end of war ; for arms and war are one
and the same thing. . . .

D.Q., I, 4, x.

* * *

. . . Learning urges that, without it, warfare itself could
not subsist ; because war, as other things, has its laws, and
is governed by them, and laws are the province of learning
and scholars. To this objection the soldiers make answer,
that without them the laws cannot be maintained, for
it is by arms that commonwealths are defended ; kingdoms,
monarchies, cities, the roads by land and the waters of the sea,
would be subject to the ravages and confusion that attends war
while it lasts, and is at liberty to make use of its unbounded
power and prerogative. Besides, it is past all controversy that
what costs dearest is, and ought to be, most valued. So for
a man to attain to an eminent degree of learning costs him time,

watching, hunger, nakedness, dizziness in the head, weakness in the stomach, and other inconveniences which are the consequences of these. . . . But the rising gradually to be a good soldier is purchased at the whole expense of all that is required for learning, and that in so surpassing a degree that there is no comparison betwixt them ; because the soldier is every moment in danger of his life. To what danger or distress can a scholar be reduced equal to that of a soldier, who, being besieged in some strong place, and at his post or upon guard in some ravelin or bastion, perceives the enemy carrying on a mine under him, and yet must upon no account remove himself from thence, or shun the danger which threatens him so near ? All he can do is to give notice to his commander that he may countermine, but himself must stand still, fearing and expecting, when on a sudden he shall soar to the clouds without wings, and be again cast down headlong against his will.

D.Q., 1, 4, xi.

* * *

Blessed be those happy ages that were strangers to the dreadful fury of these devilish instruments of artillery, whose inventor, I am satisfied, is now in Hell, receiving the reward of his cursed invention, which is the cause that very often a cowardly, base hand takes away the life of the bravest gentleman, and that in the midst of that vigour and resolution which animates and inflames the bold, a chance bullet (shot perhaps by one that fled, and was frightened at the very flash the mischievous piece gave when it went off), coming nobody knows how or from whence, in a moment puts a period to the brave designs and the life of one that deserved to have survived many years.

D.Q., 1, 4, xi.

* * *

What satisfaction in this world, what pleasure, can equal that of vanquishing and triumphing over one's enemy ?

D.Q., 1, 3, iv.

* * *

The soldier who puts his captain's command into execution may be said to do as much, at least, as the captain who commanded him.

D.Q., I, 2, v.

* * *

The wounds which we receive in combat rather add to our honour than deprive us of it.

D.Q., I, 3, i.

* * *

There is nothing so subject to the inconstancy of fortune as war.

D.Q., I, I, viii.

* * *

All laws, whether of God or man, allow one to stand in his own defence, if any offer to do him a mischief.

D.Q., I, I, viii.

* * *

The exercise of arms requires the help of the mind as well as does learning.

D.Q., I, 4, x.

* * *

Peace is the true end of war . . .

D.Q., I, 4, x.

* * *

The soldier's life is not so free . . . as not to involve more of subjection than liberty.

E.N., *The Little Gypsy Girl*.

* * *

The fame which is won in war, being engraved upon sheets of bronze with points of steel, is more stable than other forms of renown.

P.S., IV, i.

* * *

Happy the soldier who, in the midst of the fight, knows that
his leader is watching him.

P.S., IV, i.

* * *

Happy would the warring king be who should have in his
army ten thousand soldier-lovers who should look forward to
the reward of their victories being the possession of their
mistresses.

E.N., *The Spanish-English Lady*.

* * *

War, just as it is the stepmother of cowards, is a mother to
the brave, and the prizes which are won by its means can be
described as surpassing all worldly goods.

P.S., II, xii.

* * *

As the business of war is not to be compassed without vast
toil and labour, so the religious soldier must undoubtedly be
preferred before the religious monk, who, living still, quiet, and
at ease, has nothing to do but pray for the afflicted and distressed.

D.Q., I, 2, v.

* * *

There is no better sanctuary than that afforded by the house
of the enemy himself.

P.S., I, v.

* * *

It would be a pretty piece of wisdom, truly, should those out
of the town of Reloxa sally out every day on those who spend
their ill-natured breaths miscalling them everywhere. It would
be a fine business, indeed, if the inhabitants of those several
famous towns that are nick-named by our rabble, and called
the one cheesemongers, the other costermongers, these fish-
mongers, and those soap-boilers, should know no better than to
think themselves dishonoured, and in revenge be always drawing

out their swords at the least word, for every idle, insignificant quarrel. No, no, Heaven forbid !

D.Q., II, xxvii.

* * *

. . . He that cannot receive an affront consequently can give none. Women, children, and churchmen, as they cannot vindicate themselves when they are injured, so neither are they capable of receiving an affront ; for there is this difference between an affront and an injury . . . an affront must come from a person that is both able to give it and maintain it when he has given it. An injury may be done by any sort of people whatsoever : for example, a man walking in the street about his business is set upon by ten armed men who cudgel him. He draws his sword to avenge the injury, but, the assailants overpowering him, he cannot have the satisfaction he desired. This man is injured, but not affronted. But to confirm it by another instance : suppose a man comes behind another's back, hits him a box on the ear, and then runs away ; the other follows him but can't overtake him. He that has received the blow has received an injury, it is true, but not an affront ; because to make it an affront, it should have been justified. But if he that gave it, though he did it basely, stands his ground, and faces his adversary, then he that received is both injured and affronted ; injured because he was struck in a cowardly manner, affronted, because he that struck him stood his ground to maintain what he had done.

D.Q., II, xxxii.

* * *

It is neither a Christian-like nor an honourable action for men to be the butchers and tormentors of one another.

D.Q., I, 3, viii.

* * *

LOVE AND MARRIAGE

To an enemy in flight a bridge of silver ; and it is commonly said that the most formidable enemy a man has is his wife.

P.S., III, vii.

* * *

The just and due pleasure which married couples enjoy agrees with the sacrament of marriage . . . if it is wanting, the marriage is lame and renounces its second intention, since to think that an ugly face which is to be kept at all hours before the eyes in the parlour, at bed and board can cause pleasure . . . that I hold for almost impossible.

E.N., The Power of Blood.

* * *

The man of seventy who marries a girl of fifteen has either lost his wits, or else desires to visit the next world at the earliest possible moment.

C.I., The Jealous Old Man.

* * *

He who marries a beautiful woman dissolves his union with honour, unless Heaven comes to his aid.

C.I., The Fortunate Ruffian.

* * *

Rich men should not seek money in their marriages but satisfaction, for satisfaction prolongs life, while unhappiness between married people shortens it.

E.N., The Jealous Extremaduran.

* * *

Good or bad luck dominates all our actions in this life, and none more so than our marriages.

P.S., iv, i.

* * *

As it is very improper to leave an army without a general, and a garrison without its governor, so, to me, it seems much more imprudent to leave a young married woman without her husband ; especially when there are no affairs of consequence to account for his absence.

D.Q., I, 4, vii.

* * *

In well-ordered kingdoms and states, the duration of marriages would be limited, and marriages would be dissolved or confirmed anew every three years, as is the case with leases.

C.I., *The Divorce Judge*.

* * *

The worst reconciliation is preferable to the best divorce.

C.I., *Ibid*.

* * *

I have heard it said that there is a law which decrees that a husband may divorce his wife, and a wife her husband, if she, or he, as the case may be, has a bad breath.

C.I., *Ibid*.

* * *

The honour of a married man is of so nice and tender a nature that it has been sometimes sullied by the conversation of the nearest relations, and is therefore more liable to suffer from that of a friend.

D.Q., I, 4, vi.

* * *

The greatest obstacle to love is want and a narrow fortune ; for the continual bands and cements of mutual affection are mirth, content, satisfaction, and jollity. These, managed with skilful hands, can make variety in the pleasures of wedlock, preparing the same thing always with some additional circumstance, to render it new and delightful. But when pressing necessity and indigence deprive us of those pleasures that prevent satiety, the yoke of matrimony is often found to be very galling, and the burden intolerable.

D.Q., II, xii.

* * *

As the whole body is affected by the pain of any one part of it, as the head will share the pain of the foot, though it never caused that pain, so is the husband affected by his wife's infamy, because she is part of him. And since all worldly honours and dishonours are derived from flesh and blood, and the scandalous baseness of an unfaithful wife proceeds from the same principle, it necessarily follows that the husband, though no party to the offence, and entirely ignorant and innocent of it, must have his share of the infamy.

D.Q., I, 4, vi.

* * *

. . . The understanding, which alone should distinguish and choose . . . is apt to be blinded or biassed by love and affection ; and matrimony is so nice and critical a point that it requires not only our own cautious management, but even the direction of a superior power to choose right. Whoever undertakes a long journey, if he be wise, makes it his business to seek out an agreeable companion. How cautious, then, should he be who is to take a journey for life, whose fellow-traveller must not part with him but at the grave ; his companion at bed and board, and sharer of all the pleasures and fatigues of his journey, as the wife must be to the husband. She is no such sort of ware that a man can get rid of when he pleases. When once *that* is purchased, no exchange, no sale, no alienation car be made ; she is an inseparable accident to man.

Marriage is a noose, which, fastened about the neck, runs the closer and fits more uneasy by our struggling to get loose : it is a Gordian knot which none can untie, and, being twisted with our thread of life, nothing but the scythe of death can sever it.

D.Q., II, xx.

* * *

Love is born and engendered in our hearts either by choice or by destiny ; that which is the work of destiny is always rated at its true value ; that which is the outcome of choice may wax or wane in proportion as the causes which prompt us to mutual love increase or diminish.

P.S., ii, vi.

* * *

In no other operations of nature are greater and more continual miracles to be seen than in those of love, for the miracles are so great in number and of such a kind that they are passed over in silence and without notice, however astounding they may be. Love unites sceptre and crook, high with low estate, it makes the impossible possible, levels differences of rank, and comes to be as powerful as death.

P.S., I, xxiii.

* * *

The lover must not seek to endear himself by means of another's charms ; those which he displays to his lady must be his own ; if he does not sing well, he should not introduce her to a good singer ; if he is not especially handsome, let him not appear in the company of Ganymede ; and, finally, I think that he should not seek to amend any faults he may possess with the superfluous graces of others.

P.S., III, i.

* * *

Never ought lovers to say that they are poor, because, from the start, poverty is a great enemy of love.

E.N., *The Little Gypsy Girl.*

* * *

O mighty power of love, of, I say, heedless, hasty, lascivious, and ill-intentioned love ! With what ease dost thou overthrow worthy designs, chaste purposes, discreet proposals !

P.S., iii, vi.

* * *

There is no lover but, being in possession of his loved one, does not fear to lose her ; there is no venture so certain but that it may, perhaps, be accompanied by ups-and-downs of fortune ; there is no spike strong enough to halt the wheel of fortune.

P.S., iii, xix.

* * *

Sins of sensuality, for the most part, do not aim at anything much beyond the limit of their gratification.

E.N., *The Power of Blood.*

* * *

Amorous passions resemble indiscreet impulses that unhinge the will, which, falling foul of inconveniences, violently hurls itself after its desire, and thinking to meet the glory of its eyes, encounters the Hell of its sorrows. If it attains what it desires, the desire decays with the possession of the thing desired, and perchance the eyes of the understanding at length opening, it perceives it to be well that it should abhor what it hitherto adored.

E.N., *The Little Gypsy Girl.*

* * *

4

Love is a power too strong to be overcome by anything but flight.

D.Q., I, 4, vii.

* * *

The best and most dutiful servant of love's retinue is occasion or opportunity.

D.Q., I, 4, vii.

* * *

It is said of love that it sometimes goes, sometimes flies ; runs with one, walks gravely with another ; turns a third into ice, and sets a fourth in a flame.

D.Q., I, 4, vii.

* * *

The profession of a bawd, pimp, or messenger of love is not like other common employments, but an office that requires a great deal of prudence and sagacity ; an office of trust and weight, and most highly necessary in a well-regulated commonwealth ; nor should it be executed but by civil, well-descended persons of good natural parts and a liberal education. Nay, it were necessary that there should be a comptroller and surveyor of the profession, as there are of others ; and a certain and settled number of them, as there are of stockbrokers. This would be a means to prevent an infinite number of mischiefs that happen every day, because the trade or profession is followed by poor ignorant pretenders, silly waiting-women, young giddy-brained pages, shallow footmen, and such raw, inexperienced sort of people, who in unexpected turns and emergencies stand with their fingers in their mouths, know not their right hand from their left, but suffer themselves to be surprised, and spoil all for want of quickness of invention either to conceal, carry on, or bring off a thing skilfully.

D.Q., I, 3, viii.

* * *

All these stories of people dying for love are tales of a roasted horse. They tell you they will die for love, but the devil a bit.

D.Q., ii, lxx.

* * *

Slights and disdain are wont to kill love in its early stages because they deprive it of the support of hope, which causes love to increase.

P.S., ii, xix.

* * *

Once love has taken full and entire possession of the soul, disdain and disillusion serve as spurs to make it run faster, so that it may transform its thoughts into action.

P.S., iv, iii.

* * *

Love is void of consideration, and disclaims the rules of reason in his proceedings. He is like death, and equally assaults the lofty palaces of kings, and the lowly cottages of shepherds. Wherever he takes entire possession of the soul, the first thing he does is to banish thence all bashfulness and shame.

D.Q., ii, lviii.

* * *

THE FEMALE OF THE SPECIES

The weakest part of woman is her vanity.

D.Q., I, 4, vi.

* * *

That is the nature of women, not to love when we love them, and to love when we love them not.

D.Q., I, 3, vi.

* * *

There is as good bread baked here as in France, and Joan is as good as my lady, in the dark.

D.Q., II, xxxiii.

* * *

Levity and vanity of mind is natural to womankind.

D.Q., I, 4, xxiv.

* * *

Between a woman's " yes " and " nay " I would not engage to put a pin's point, so close they be to one another.

D.Q., II, xix.

* * *

Public reputation is the life of a lady's virtue, and the outward appearance of modesty is in one sense as good as the reality ; since a private sin is not so prejudicial in this world as a public indecency.

D.Q., II, xxii.

* * *

When once a woman parts with her virtue, she loses the esteem even of the man whose vows and tears won her to abandon it.

D.Q., I, 4 vii

* * *

There are no guards, bolts, or locks which preserve a young woman like her own caution.

D.Q., I, 4, xxiv.

* * *

There is no load heavier than a light woman.

P.S., IV, i.

* * *

The best dowry which a gentlewoman can possess is virtue, for beauty and riches are ravaged by time.

P.S., IV, i.

* * *

A good woman is . . . not unlike a mirror of crystal, which will infallibly be dimmed and stained by breathing too much upon it.

E.N., *The Dialogue of the Dogs.*

* * *

A modest and honest woman is the most valuable jewel in the world, so all women's virtue and honour consist in the opinion and reputation they maintain with other people.

D.Q., I, 4, vi.

* * *

The modest maid and a broken leg should stay at home.

D.Q., II, xlix.

* * *

The woman and the hen are lost by gadding.

D.Q., ii, xlix.

* * *

She who desires to see desires no less to be seen.

D.Q., ii, xlix.

* * *

It is no treat, but a trial, to kiss an old woman and let her kiss you.

E.N., *The Dialogue of the Dogs.*

* * *

" Since nothing is frailer than woman and glass,
He that would expose them to fall is an ass ;
And sure the rash mortal is yet more unwise,
Who, on bodies so ticklish, experiments tries.

" With ease both are damaged ; then keep that with care,
Which no art can restore, nor no solder repair.
Fond man, take my counsel, watch what is so frail ;
For where Danäes lie, golden showers will prevail."

E.N., *ibid.*

* * *

The addresses and services of an importunate lover are the mire into which you should never drive a woman.

E.N., *ibid.*

* * *

A celebrated poet of our time wrote a very scurrilous and abusive lampoon upon all the intriguing ladies of the Court, forbearing to name one, as not being sure whether she deserved to be put into the catalogue or not ; but the lady, not finding herself there, was not a little affronted at the omission, and

made a great complaint to the poet, asking him what he had
seen in her that he should leave her out of his list, and desiring
him at the same time to enlarge his satire, and put her in, or
expect to hear further from her. The author obeyed her
commands, and gave her a character with a vengeance, and, to
her great satisfaction, made her as famous for infamy as any
woman about the town.

D.Q., II, viii.

* * *

Many faults are concealed by good breeding, lavish adornment
of the person, and magnificent furnishings of the house ; for
it is impossible that good breeding should offend, or that lavish
adornment should fail to give satisfaction. Hippolyta, a courte-
san, had all these things and could compete in riches with Flora
of the ancient world, and in manners with good breeding itself.
It was impossible for anyone who knew her to think little of
her, for her beauty cast a spell on all and her wealth brought
her esteem, and her courtesy rendered her, if one may so phrase
it, meet to be adored. When love invests itself with these three
qualities it breaks hearts of bronze, opens purses of iron, and
conquers wills of marble ; and, especially, if to these three
things are added deceit and flattery, attributes appropriate to
those who desire to exhibit their charms in the light of the
world.

P.S., IV, vii.

* * *

A handsome, brisk, young, rich widow, and withal no prude,
happened to fall in love with a well-set, lusty lay-brother. His
superior, hearing of it, took occasion to go to her, and said to
her, by way of charitable admonition, " I mightily wonder,
madam, how a lady of your merit, so admired for beauty and
for sense, and withal so rich, could make so ill a choice, and
dote on a mean, silly, despicable fellow, as I hear you do, while
we have in our house so many masters of arts, bachelors, and
doctors of divinity among whom your ladyship may pick and

choose, as you would among pears, and say, ' This I like, that
I do not like.' " But she answered the officious, grave gentleman :
" Sir," said she, with a smile, " you are much mistaken, and
think altogether after the old-fashioned way, if you imagine
that I have made so ill a choice ; for though you fancy the man
is a fool, yet as to what I take him for, he knows as much, or
rather more, philosophy than Aristotle himself.

D.Q., I, 3, xi

* * *

Foolish, illiterate women, footmen, and cobblers pretend
nowadays to draw certainties from the stars, as easily and readily
as they shuffle a pack of cards.

D.Q., II, xxv

* * *

Sure it is impossible that an antiquated lady-in-waiting, in a
long white veil, like a winding sheet, with a pair of spectacles
on her nose, should create, or waken, an unchaste thought in
the most abandoned libertine in the world. Is there any of
these duennas, or governesses, that has good flesh ? Is there
one of these implements of antechambers that is not impertinent,
affected, and intolerable ? Avaunt then, all ye idle crowd of
wrinkled female waiters, unfit for any human recreation !

D.Q., II, xlviii

* * *

There is no virtue but is enclosed within the stays of a lady-
in-waiting.

D.Q., II, xxxvi

* * *

Where there are old waiting-women, good fortune can happen
cie to no man.

D.Q., II, xxxvi

* * *

SANCHO PANZA, GOVERNOR, PASSES JUDGMENT

In came a woman, hauling along a man that looked like a good, substantial grazier. "Justice, my Lord Governor, justice!" cried she aloud; "and if I cannot have it on earth, I will have it from Heaven! Sweet Lord Governor, this wicked fellow met me in the middle of a field, and has had the full use of my body; he has handled me like a dish-clout. Woe is me, he has robbed me of that which I had kept these three-and-twenty years. Wretch that I am, I had guarded it safe from natives and foreigners, Christians and infidels! I have been always as tough as a cork; no salamander ever kept itself more entire in fire, nor no wool among the briers, than I did, poor I, till this lewd man with dirty fists handled me at this rate." "Woman, woman," quoth Sancho, "no reflections yet; whether your gallant's hands were dirty or clean, that is not to the purpose." Then, turning to the grazier, "Well friend," said he, "what have you to say to this woman's complaint?" "My Lord," answered the man, looking as if he had been frightened out of his wits, "I am a poor drover. . . . Now, as I was trudging home, whom should I pick up but this hedge-madam here; and the Devil, who has a finger in every pie, being powerful, forced us to yoke together. I gave her that which would have contented any reasonable woman; but she was not satisfied, and wanted more money; and would never leave me until she had dragged me hither. She will tell you I ravished her; but by the oath I have taken, or mean to take, she lies, like a drab that she is, and this is every tittle true."

"Fellow," quoth Sancho, "hast thou any silver about thee?" "Yes, if it please your worship," answered the drover, "I have some twenty ducats in silver, in a leathern purse here in my bosom."

"Give it the plaintiff, money and all," quoth Sancho. The man, with a trembling hand, did as he was commanded: the woman took it, and dropped a thousand courtesies to the company, wishing, on her knees, as many blessings to the good Governor, who took such special care of poor fatherless and motherless children, and abused virgins. . . .

D.Q., II, xlv.

★ ★ ★

SCANDAL AND SCANDALMONGERS

So thy conscience is clear, let the world talk at random, as it is wont to do. One may as soon tie up the winds as the tongues of slanderers. If a governor returns rich from his government, they say he has fleeced and robbed the people ; if poor, then they call him idle, a fool, and a wastrel.

D.Q., II, lv.

* * *

The more eminently virtue shines, the more it is exposed to the persecution of envy. Few or none of the famous heroes of antiquity could escape the venomous arrows of calumny. Julius Caesar, that most courageous, prudent, and valiant captain, was marked as being ambitious, and neither so clean in his apparel, nor in his manners, as he ought to have been. Alexander, whose mighty deeds gained him the title of the Great, was charged with being addicted to drunkenness. Hercules, after his many heroic labours, was accused of voluptuousness and effeminacy.

D.Q., II, ii.

* * *

In the country, and in our little towns, there is not the least thing can be said or done, but people will talk and find fault.

D.Q., I, 2, iv.

* * *

When any gentleman at a bull-fight gives the bull a home thrust with his lance, or when anybody behaves himself skilfully upon any occasion, the people will cry out, "What a brisk son of a whore that is ! A clever dog, I will warrant him !" So what seems to be slander, in that sense is notable commendation.

D.Q., II, xiii.

* * *

There are many divines that could make but very dull preachers, and yet are quick at finding faults and superfluities in other men's sermons.

D.Q., II, iii.

* * *

Let every man mind his own business and give good words, or hold his tongue.

D.Q., I, 3, viii.

* * *

Those who will play with cats must expect to be scratched.

D.Q., I, 3, viii.

* * *

A stink is stlil worse for the stirring.

D.Q., I, 4, xxii.

* * *

Doing and speaking evil we inherit from our first parents, and suck them in with our mother's milk. It is clearly seen in that when the child has scarcely taken its arm out of the swaddling clothes, it lifts its hand, and shows signs of desiring to revenge itself upon him whom it supposes to have offended it, and almost the first articulate word it utters is in blame of its nurse or its mother.

E.N., *The Dialogue of the Dogs.*

* * *

Slander has no greater veil to palliate and conceal its dissolute wickedness than for the slanderer to suppose that all he says consists of sentences of philosophy, and that to speak ill is reprehension, and to disclose the shortcomings of others is righteous zeal. There is no life of any censorious person that, if you consider and pry into it, you do not find full of vice and insolence.

E.N., *The Dialogue of the Dogs.*

* * *

A slanderous tongue is like a two-edged sword which cuts right through to the bone, or like a thunderbolt from heaven which, without smashing the sheath, breaks and destroys the steel which it covers. And although conversations and social functions derive savour from the salt of gossip, nevertheless they tend, in the majority of cases, to be accompanied by a bitter and unsavoury after-taste. The tongue is as light as thought, and, if the pregnancies of thought are evil, the parturitions of the tongue make them yet worse ; and as words are like pebbles thrown by the hand, which objects cannot be recalled, nor can they return to the place from which they came until they have had their effect, on few occasions does remorse for having uttered them lessen the guilt of the person who did so, although I have already observed that hearty repentance is the best medicine for the ills of the soul.

P.S., i, xiv.

* * *

Watch over your tongue, for in it lie the greatest misfortunes of human life.

E.N., *The Dialogue of the Dogs.*

* * *

If all rulers were to busy themselves in performing good works, nobody would be concerned to speak ill of them ; but why should he who does ill expect to be well spoken of ? And if virtuous works, well done, are denigrated by human malice, why should not evil works meet with the same fate ? Why should he who sows wild oats and evil, expect good fruit as his reward ?

P.S., i, xvi.

* * *

As for old gossips, the older they are the more their tongues wag, for they have seen more, and all the pleasures of all the other senses have been concentrated upon, and confined to, the tongue.

P.S., i, xviii.

* * *

Nobody should be so rash as to make known in public faults committed in secret, especially those of the kings and princes who govern us ; a private person has no business to reprimand his king and lord, nor bring the faults of a prince to the ears of his vassals, because this will not have the effect of improving him but will rather cause his household to despise him ; and if correction ought to be fraternal and mutual, why should not the prince enjoy this privilege ? Why should his faults be thrown publicly in his face ? For it is possible that public and ill-considered reprimand is wont to strengthen the disposition of the one who receives it, and to make him obstinate rather than compliant ; and as it is inevitable that both true and imagined faults should be the object of blame, nobody wishes to be chided in public, and satirical persons, slanderers, and the malicious are sent into exile and ejected from their homes, without honour and with vituperation ; the only commendation remaining to them is that they are dubbed wits as well as knaves, and knaves as well as wits, and it comes to pass, as common parlance has it, that treachery pleases, while the traitor irritates.

P.S., i, xiv.

* * *

An ounce of public dishonour is a more grievous burthen than five-and-twenty pounds of secret infamy.

E.N., *The Power of Blood.*

* * *

VIRTUE, FREEDOM, AND COURAGE

Virtue and right understanding remain always the same; naked or clothed, alone or accompanied. It is quite true, they may suffer in the estimation of the crowd, but not in the true reality of their worth and value.

E.N., *The Dialogue of the Dogs.*

* * *

It seems that good and evil are so little distant from one another that they may be compared with two converging lines which, although they start from different and separate beginnings, end at the same point.

P.S., IV, xii.

* * *

It is the part of noble and generous spirits to pass by trifles.

D.Q., I, 3, vi.

* * *

Humility is the base and foundation of all the virtues and . . . without it there is none that is virtue. It smooths away obstacles, it conquers difficulties, it is one means that always conduces to glorious ends. Of enemies it makes friends, it tempers the anger of the impetuous, and it diminishes the arrogance of the proud. It is the mother of modesty and the sister of moderation. In short, with it vices cannot secure a triumph which will be profitable to them, because on its suavity and mildness the darts of sin are blunted and lose their points.

E.N., *The Dialogue of the Dogs.*

* * *

Liberty is one of the most valuable blessings that Heaven has bestowed on mankind. Not all the treasures concealed in the bowels of the earth, nor those in the bosom of the sea, can be compared with it. For liberty, a man may, nay, ought to, hazard even his life, as well as for honour, accounting captivity the greatest misery he can endure.

D.Q., ii, lviii.

* * *

One man is no more than another if he does no more than another.

D.Q., i, 3, v.

* * *

We are only to relieve the afflicted, to look on their distress, and not on their crimes.

D.Q., i, 4, iii.

* * *

We ought to love our Maker for His own sake, without either hope of good or fear of pain.

D.Q., i, 4, iv.

* * *

The path of virtue is narrow, and the way of vice easy and open ; but their ends and resting-places are very different. The latter is a broad road indeed, and down-hill all the way, but death and contempt are always met at the end of the journey ; whereas the former leads to glory and life, not a life that soon must have an end, but an immortal being.

D.Q., ii, vi.

* * *

" Thro' steep ascents, thro' straight and rugged ways,
Ourselves to glory's lofty seats we raise ;
In vain he hopes to reach the bless'd abode,
Who leaves the narrow path for the more easy road."

D.Q., II, vi.

* * *

DUTIES OF A KNIGHT-ERRANT

. . . Our greatest foes, and whom we must chiefly combat, are within. Envy we must overcome by generosity and nobleness of soul ; anger by a reposed and easy mind ; riot and sluggishness by vigilance and temperance ; lasciviousness, by our inviolable fidelity to those who are mistresses of our thoughts ; and sloth, by our indefatigable peregrinations through the universe to seek occasions of military as well as Christian honours. This is the road to lasting fame, and a good and honourable renown.

D.Q., II, viii.

* * *

All men cannot be monks ; we have different paths allotted to us to mount to the high seat of eternal felicity.

D.Q., II, viii.

* * *

To withdraw is not to run away, and to stay is no wise action where there is more reason to fear than to hope. It is the part of a wise man to keep himself to-day for to-morrow, and not venture all his eggs in one basket.

D.Q., I, 3, ix.

* * *

Even cowards and men of little courage are daring and insolent when they are favoured, and hasten to insult those who are of greater worth than they.

E.N., *The Dialogue of the Dogs*.

* * *

In situations of extreme danger all reason is cast to the winds, no position of respect is worth anything, and no proper bounds are kept.

P.S., II, xvi.

* * *

Valour lies just half-way between rashness and cowardice.

D.Q., II, iv.

* * *

Courage which has not wisdom for its guide falls under the name of temerity, and the rash man's successful actions are rather owing to his good fortune than to his bravery.

D.Q., II, xxviii.

* * *

When the valiant man flies, he must have discovered some foul play, and it is the part of prudent persons to reserve themselves for more favourable opportunities.

D.Q., II, xxviii.

* * *

Rashness is not courage. While there is any hope, we are permitted to be bold, but not desperate.

D.Q., II, lxiii.

* * *

RICHES AND POVERTY

I had rather munch a crust of brown bread and an onion in a corner, without any more ado and ceremony, than feed upon turkey at another man's table.

D.Q., I, 2, iii.

* * *

A poor man is scarce noticed, but everyone's eyes will stare upon the rich.

D.Q., II, v.

* * *

There is no sauce in the world like hunger ; and as the poor never want that, they always eat with a good stomach.

D.Q., II, v.

* * *

The advice of the poor man, however good it may be, is never accepted, nor is the humble and poor man to have the presumption to counsel the great and those who think that they know everything. Knowledge in the poor man is under a cloud, for necessity and poverty are shadows and clouds that obscure it, and if it is perchance discovered, men judge it folly and treat it with contempt.

E.N., *The Dialogue of the Dogs.*

* * *

An alms of two *maravedis* cheerfully bestowed upon an indigent beggar, by a man in poor circumstances, speaks him as liberal as the larger gift of a vainglorious rich man before a fawning crowd.

D.Q., II, vii.

* * *

The poor man whom virtue enriches is wont to attain fame, just as the rich man, if he is vicious, can attain, and does attain, infamy ; liberality is one of the most agreeable of the virtues and it engenders a good name ; this is so true, that no generous man is badly placed in life, just as there is no avaricious man who is not badly situated.

P.S., II, xiv.

* * *

Those who are born of humble parents rarely, unless heaven grants them extremely powerful aid, rise by their own efforts to positions in which they are singled out for the public gaze ; if, that is, virtue does not lend them a generous hand.

P.S., II, v.

* * *

Among the poor, friendships can be lasting because equality of fortune serves to bind souls together ; but there cannot be enduring friendship between rich and poor on account of the inequality which exists between wealth and poverty.

P.S., II, v.

* * *

Have no desires, and you will be the richest man in the world.

P.S., IV, i.

* * *

Poverty may partly eclipse a gentleman, but cannot totally obscure him.

D.Q., II (Preface).

* * *

How miserable is a poor gentleman who, to keep up his honour, starves his person, fares sorrily, or fasts unseen within his solitary, narrow apartment ; then, putting the best face he can upon the matter, comes out picking his teeth, though it is but an honourable hypocrisy, and though he has eaten nothing that requires that nice exercise ! Unhappy he, whose honour is in continual alarms, who thinks that at a mile's distance everyone discovers the patch in his shoes, the sweat of his forehead soaked through his old rusty hat, the threadbareness of his clothes, and the very hunger of his famished stomach.

D.Q., II, xlv.

* * *

The rich man's follies pass for wise sayings, in this world.

D.Q., II, xliii.

* * *

Not he who possesses, but he that spends and enjoys his wealth, is the rich and happy man.

D.Q., II, vii.

* * *

PROSPERITY AND ADVERSITY

Fortune is a whimsical, freakish, drunken quean, and blind into the bargain ; so that she neither sees what she does, nor knows whom she raises, nor whom she casts down.

D.Q., ii, lxvi.

* * *

How hard a thing it is to endure the passage from a happy state to an unhappy. . . . When miseries and misfortunes swell the volume of the current, and are continuous, either they are speedily terminated by death or the continuation of them creates a habit and custom of enduring them which in their greatest severity serves as an alleviation ; but when, from an ill-starred and calamitous fortune, we, without anticipating it and unexpectedly, rise to the enjoyment of another prosperous, fortunate, and agreeable destiny, and upon that there ensues in a little time a return to suffering the original lot and the original troubles and mischances, it is sorrow so bitter that if it does not put an end to life, to live longer is only to exacerbate it.

E.N., *The Dialogue of the Dogs.*

* * *

The security in which human pleasures are enjoyed is so insignificant that nobody can be assured of the slightest degree of stability for them.

P.S., iv, xiv.

* * *

I cannot endure or tolerate patiently the complaints I hear some men utter concerning fortune, when the best that they aspired to was to entertain claims and hopes to be pages.

E.N., *The Dialogue of the Dogs.*

* * *

Troubles, toils, and disappointments add a cipher to the years, and mayhap two, according as one fancies.

E.N., *The Jealous Extremaduran.*

* * *

A humble lot was never bettered by ease or idleness ; good fortune never took up its abode in faint and withered hearts ; we ourselves are the architects of our own fate, and no soul exists but it is capable of raising itself to its proper place ; cowards, although they may be born rich, are always poor, as misers are always beggars.

P.S., II, xii.

* * *

It is as much the part of great spirits to have patience when the world frowns upon them, as to be joyful when all goes well.

D.Q., II, lxvi.

* * *

He that is down to-day may be up to-morrow, unless he has a mind to lie a-bed.

D.Q., II, lv.

* * *

Fortune turns round like a mill-wheel, and he that was yesterday at the top, lies to-day at the bottom.

D.Q., I, 4, xx.

* * *

The brave man carves out his fortune, and every man is the son of his own works.

D.Q., I, I, iv.

* * *

Many think to find flitches of bacon where there is not so much as the racks to lay them on.

D.Q., I, 3, xi.

*　*　*

Delay breeds danger ; and when a cow be given thee, run and halter her.

D.Q., II, xlii.

*　*　*

In our disasters, fortune leaves always some door open to come at a remedy.

D.Q., I, 3, i.

*　*　*

The bitch fortune is still unkind to men of wit.

D.Q., I, 3, viii.

*　*　*

Those who follow their nose are often led into a stink.

D.Q., II, xiii.

*　*　*

Misfortunes seek out and find the unfortunate being, even if he hide himself in the furthest corner of the world.

E.N., *The Dialogue of the Dogs.*

*　*　*

It is one thing to praise discipline, and another to submit to it.

E.N., *The Dialogue of the Dogs.*

*　*　*

Extreme affliction often distracts the mind to that degree, and so deprives us of memory, that sometimes we for a while can scarce think on our very names.

D.Q., I, 4, iii.

* * *

SLEEP AND DEATH

There is very little difference between a man in his first sleep and a man in his last sleep.

D.Q., ii, lxviii.

* * *

There is no remembrance which time will not deface, nor no pain to which death will not put a period.

D.Q., i, 3, i.

* * *

Death is very ugly, and that which most closely approaches it is disease ; and to love ugly things smacks of the supernatural and is worthy to be regarded as a miracle.

P.S., iv, ix.

* * *

There is a remedy for everything except death, especially if you can, or care to, be silent.

E.N., *The Jealous Extremaduran.*

* * *

Death is deaf, and when he knocks at the door, mercy on the porter.

D.Q., ii, vii.

* * *

. . . A comedy is acted on the great stage of the world, where some play the emperors, others the prelates, and, in short, all the parts can be brought into a dramatic piece ; till death, which is the catastrophe and end of the action, strips the actors of all their marks of distinction, and levels their quality in the grave.

D.Q., ii, xii.

* * *

Now blessings light upon him that first invented sleep ; it covers a man all over, thoughts and all, like a cloak ; it is meat for the hungry, drink for the thirsty, heat for the cold, and cold for the hot. It is the current coin that purchases all the pleasures of the world cheap ; and the balance that sets the king and the shepherd, the fool and the wise man, even.

D.Q., ii, lxviii.

* * *

When the hour is come we must all be packed off, the prince and the peasant go the same way at last ; the road is no fairer for one than the other. The Pope's body takes up no more room than the sexton's, though one be taller.

D.Q., ii, xxxiii.

* * *

Death and sleep make us all alike, rich and poor, high and low.

D.Q., ii, xliii.

* * *

Sleep with moderation ; for he that rises not with the sun loses so much day.

D.Q., ii, xliii.

* * *

It is the maddest trick a man can ever play in his whole life, to let his breath sneak out of his body without any more ado, and without so much as a rap over the pate, or a kick in the guts ; to go out like the snuff of a farthing candle, and die merely of the mulligrubs, or the sullens.

D.Q., ii, lxxiv.

* * *

There is a strange charm in the thoughts of a good legacy, or the hopes of an estate, which wondrously removes, or at least alleviates, the sorrow that men would otherwise feel for the death of their friends.

D.Q., II, lxxiv.

* * *

. . . All human things, especially the lives of men, are transitory, their very beginnings being but steps to their dissolution.

D.Q., II, lxxiv.

* * *

Death eats up all things, both the young lamb and the old sheep ; and I have heard our parson say, death values a prince no more than a clown ; all is fish that comes to his net ; he throws at all, and sweeps the stakes ; he is no mower that takes a nap at noon-day, but drives on, fair weather or foul, and cuts down the green grass as well as the ripe corn : he is neither squeamish nor queasy-stomached, for he swallows without chewing, and crams down all things into his ungracious maw ; and though you can see he has no belly, he has a confounded dropsy, and thirsts after men's lives, which he guzzles down like mother's milk.

D.Q., II, xx.

* * *

A FEW OF SANCHO PANZA'S PROVERBS

Better my daughter ill married than well kept.

He who will not when he may, when he will he shall have nay.

> "The wife that expects to have a good name
> Is always at home as if she were lame ;
> And the maid that is honest, her chiefest delight
> Is still to be doing from morning till night."

There is no friend : all friendship is gone ; now men hug, then fight anon.

No man knows what another can do ; so let every man's choler sleep with him.

A good paymaster needs no surety.

Sancho the squire may sooner get to Heaven than Sancho the governor.

In the night all cats are grey.

Unhappy is he who wants his breakfast at two in the afternoon.

The sparrow speeds as well as the sparrow-hawk.

Good serge is fine ; but coarse cloth is warm, and four yards of one are as long as four yards of the other.

There can be no mischief sure where there is music.

A golden load makes the burden light.

Scratch my backside and I will claw your elbow.

There is a time for some things, and a time for all things ; a time for great things, and a time for small things.

In a rich man's house the cloth is soon laid.

Store's no sore.

He who rings the bells is safe.

What a man has, so much he is sure of.

Whom God loves, his house happy proves.

Between two cheek-teeth never clap thy thumbs.

He that gives a broken head can give a plaster.

This is one day, but to-morrow is another.

Strange things may fall out in the roasting of an egg.

eaven knows the truth of all things.

he Devil lurks behind the Cross.

Welcome ill-luck when it comes alone.

Where there is no hook, to be sure there will hang no bacon.

he hare leaps out of the bush when we least look for her.

little in one's own pocket is better than much in another man's
arse.

While a man gets he never can lose.

aper speaks when beards never wag.

oney is not made for an ass's mouth.

is best grinding at the mill before the water is past.

o the grave with the dead, and the living to the bread.

hat man loves thee well who makes thee to weep.

ever cringe nor creep for what you by force may reap.

leap from a hedge is better than the prayer of a good man.

t him that owns the cow take her by the tail.

closed mouth catches no flies.

is a sorry goose that will not baste herself.

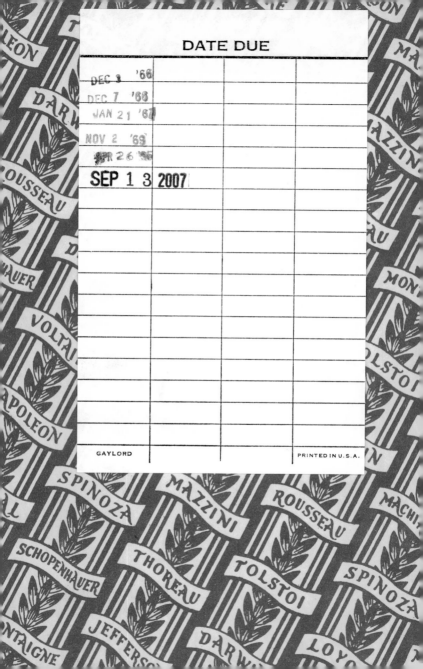